Meadowlark Economics

Meadowlark Economics

Perspectives on Ecology, Work, and Learning

James Eggert

M. E. Sharpe Inc.
Armonk, New York • London, England

Available in the United Kingdom and Europe from M. E. Sharpe,
Publishers, 3 Henrietta Street, London WC2E 8LU.

First printing 1992

Library of Congress Cataloguing-in-Publication Data

Eggert, Jim. 1943-
  Meadowlark economics : perspectives on ecology, work, and learning
/ by James Eggert.
              p. cm.
  Includes bibliographical references and index.
  ISBN 1-56324-163-3 (paperback)
  1. Economic development—Environmental aspects. 2. Environmental
policy. 3. Environmental protection. 4. Human ecology. I. Title.
HD75.6.E.35 1992
  363.7—dc20   92-17735
                                                          CIP

Printed in the United States of America

The paper used in this publication meets the minimum requirements of
the American National Standards for Information Sciences—Permanence
of Paper for Printed Library Materials, ANSI Z 39.48—1984.

HA   10 9 8 7 6 5 4 3 2 1

   The book is printed on recycled paper.

To my brother Rich,
plus Dick Damro and John Medelman—a trio
of surprise and fond memories

"Meadowlark Economics" reprinted by permission from *Challenge, The Magazine of Economic Affairs*, M. E. Sharpe, September/October 1991 (Armonk, NY). Originally a briefer version was published in *The Washington Post*, August 4, 1991, under the title "A Silence of Meadowlarks."

"Craftsmanship and Salvation," first published in *Jump River Review*, March 1981 (Wausau, WI).

"Less-Dependent Workers," first published in *North Country Anvil*, #45, Fall 1983 (Millville, MN).

"Henry Thoreau as Economic Prophet," first published in *North Country Anvil*, #33, November 1980 (Millville, MN).

"Consensus Forecasting—A Ten Year Report Card," first published in *Challenge, The Magazine of Economic Affairs*, M.E. Sharpe, July/August, 1987 (Armonk, NY).

"Pro-Growth vs. Anti-Growth," adapted from James Eggert, *Invitation to Economics*, Bristlecone/Mayfield, 1991, pp. 96-99.

"The Coming Repair Age," originally published in *Craft Report*, Vol. 7, #72, September, 1981 (Seattle, WA).

"Some Liberal Praise For Milton Freedman," adapted from "A Liberal's Guide To Milton Friedman," first published in *Coevolutionary Quarterly*, #22, Summer, 1979 (Sausalito, CA).

"Growth and Global Pollution," adapted from *Invitation to Economics*, Bristlecone/Mayfield, 1991, pp. 314-319.

"Topsoil Drama," first published in *Elementary Teachers' Ideas and Materials Workshop*, December, 1988 (Great Neck, NY).

"High Jumping," first published in *Heartland Journal* #13, Spring, 1983 (Chicago, IL).

The woodcuts used as illustrations in this book are attributed to Albrecht Dürer. See *The Complete Woodcuts of Albrecht Dürer*, edited by Willi Kurth, (New York: Dover Publications, 1963).

By the power of our imagination we can sense the future generations breathing with the rhythm of our own breath or feel them hovering like a cloud of witnesses. Sometimes I fancy that if I were to turn my head suddenly, I would glimpse them over my shoulder.[1]

—Joanna Macy

/ TABLE OF CONTENTS

Preface

/ PREFACE

When *Meadowlark Economics* first landed on my desk in manuscript form, it captured my imagination. The meadowlark's brilliant, lilting song stirs happy childhood memories of a family farm in Wisconsin. The bird's enchanting melody called me to wander into the meadow, the woods, and swamps along the edge of our eighty acres. A long lane led from our unpaved road to distant pastures. Every morning twenty milk cows trekked from barn to pasture and after grazing returned in the evening. That daily pounding of so many hooves ground the soil to fluffy powder that filled the wagon ruts on both sides of the lane. We kids loved to plotch our bare feet into those deep, cool furrows. The lark, advancing ahead of us, flitted from fence post to bush to tree, calling us forward to marshy pasture.

The summer sky shone crystal blue, with columns of cumulus clouds marching inexorably from west to east toward the distant horizon. The hot July breeze, smelling of late hay, set off waves rolling across the waist-high corn. The corn whispered in response to the sighing wind, and the lark gave counterpoint to the dialogue. The meadowlark's song and flight evokes images of man living in mutual harmony with an ordered nature—peaceful, tranquil, creative, and productive.

In reading *Meadowlark Economics*, I sensed the author shared my feelings about enjoying and preserving the natural environment. Yet this book also reveals a conflict in values that the most committed ecologist must face. Such conflict pits the powerful American values of individual freedom and rights against the values of community necessary for sustaining the environment.

Preserving the ecology has unavoidable logical consequences: individual action must be restrained and channeled in the use of air, water, soil, and other resources. It would be great if American society, families, schools, and other institutions could so educate and train people from childhood on in self-discipline and restraint, that laws, rules, incentives, and punishments administered by the community weren't necessary. Some cultures achieve this more than our own. The Japanese have an admirable ability to achieve consensus, harmony, restraint and respect in many areas of life.

But the dominant American culture seems to move in the opposite direction: individual development, independence, competition, strife. The environment exists to be exploited for personal gain. As a result, the responsibility for preservation has been delegated to the community—in the tradition of Hobbes, Locke, and the eighteenth century Enlightenment—to create a civilized society by asking individuals to surrender some of their rights and freedoms to elected government. This is essential for any society to progress on a rational path from social anarchy to harmonious civilization.

Planet Earth has now reached a new and profound stage of evolution. Our challenge is not only to sustain civil harmony and a social contract of freedom and justice, but to sustain the natural environment that nurtures human civilization itself.

For us economists, it is all too convenient to retreat into a world of narrowly constrained technical models, and thereby avoid the value-laden choices that ultimately shape the course of our economy and the larger civilization. Only when we face honestly the value conflicts involved in making such policy choices, can we resolve them. In publishing this collection of essays, M.E. Sharpe, Inc. hopes to contribute to more enlightened economic analysis and more relevant and effective policies that are good for both the economy and the global ecology.

—Richard D. Bartel
May, 1992

PART I

/ VALUES OF A DIFFERENT ORDER

/ Meadowlark Economics

f I were a CEO or the head of a government agency, I have my doubts whether I would hire a contemporary economist. This may seem like an odd comment coming from someone who has spent the past twenty-two years of his life teaching university Econ classes. Indeed, there have been countless occasions when I've defended my discipline's importance to my students and others.

What is economics' special contribution? Economists' stock-in-trade includes: recognizing scarcity; helping to make choices; identifying tradeoffs; and making connections (that may not always be obvious) between the larger economy and one's own small, individual, economic world.

On the last point, I recall a class in the mid-1980s when a student asked what I meant by "making connections." It happened on a day that Nature, fortuitously, provided me with an interesting and unusual example. I told the students that I had trouble getting to school that morning because a couple of aspen trees (near a damned-up marshy area) had been cut overnight and had blocked the roadway.

"Now what," I asked, "did international trade and finance have to do with these downed trees and my morning's frustration?" Working it through, we concluded that there, indeed, may have been connections:

—Who cut the trees? Probably beaver.

—Why were they felling trees near the road? Overpopulation.

—Why were there too many beaver? No trapping that year.

—What happened to the beaver pelt market? Decreased foreign demand.

—Why? High value of the American dollar in the spring of 1985.

Some of the fun of teaching is thinking through such illustrations, examining, as it were, the connective tissue of the Big Economy, world markets, and then trying to see how they relate to you and me. Indeed, most economists are trained to do this kind of analysis quite well.

So what's our shortcoming? I believe it is simply this: we economists have simply not gone *far enough* in broadening our understanding of ecology and ecological values.

ECOLOGY AND ECONOMICS

"Ecology." Note that the words "economics" and "ecology" have the same prefix "eco," from the Greek *oikos*, which literally means "household." Thus the original definition of economics implied an understanding, a caring for, and the management of human households, whereas ecology implied an understanding and appreciation of the interrelationships within nature's "household." I believe these two households are becoming more interdependent and their futures more and more intimately linked. When we fail to calculate ecological values or to see the connections, it paves the way for losses that are both unintended and unwanted. One example (on a small scale to be sure) is now occurring in our area, a dairy farming region of the upper Midwest. We are losing our meadowlarks!

Indeed, the people who walk or jog or bike along our rural roads enjoy the few meadowlarks that are left. Their song is pleasing, their color and swoop-of-flight is enchanting. The complete disappearance of meadowlarks would, plain and simple, be wrong ethically, and also would diminish the quality of our lives.

Why are we losing the meadowlarks? Most likely it is a result of a modern method of haying—"haylage." Farmers now tend to cut their hay "green" with minimal drying early in the spring, put it into a wagon, then blow it into the silo. Years ago, most farmers let their hay grow longer—perhaps two to three weeks longer—before cutting it. It was then dried and raked into windrows. This method gave the field nesting birds (such as the meadowlarks and bobolinks) time to establish a brood and fledge their young before the mower arrived on the scene.

Haylage in turn is an offshoot of improved farm "efficiency," of substituting machinery for labor, and of minimizing time and costly rain delays that characterized the old cutting/drying/baling method. These changes took place with the blessings of Ag economists, university researchers, on down the line to the county extension agent. But in the meantime, who was valuing the meadowlarks?

Despite their sweet song, these birds have no voice economically or politically. They represent a zero within our conventional economic accounting system (we don't even buy birdseed or build birdhouses for meadowlarks). Their disappearance would not create even the tiniest ripple in the Commerce Department's spreadsheets that are supposed to measure our standard of living.

MEADOWLARK VALUES

In truth, there are "Meadowlark Values" (as opposed to strict economic values) *everywhere*. They are found in estuaries and sand dunes, in wetlands and woodlands, in native prairies and Panamanian rainforests. It is quite probable that the quality of *your* life is, to some degree, dependent on these values; they are on every continent, they can be seen upstate and downstate. Just look about and you will find them (like our meadowlarks) on your road, or next door, or even in your own back yard.

Meadowlark Values were underrepresented when Mr. Bush's economists advised the President to open up the Arctic National Wildlife Refuge (ANWR) for oil and gas exploration. Meadowlark Values were shortchanged when economists pointed out (quite correctly) that Exxon's oil spill actually *increased* our Gross Domestic Product (GDP), (by pouring billions of dollars into the cleanup and thereby fattening paychecks as well as state and national income).

Perhaps it is time we economists begin to rethink our strict adherence to dollar and GDP values. We should not, of course, discard our old and valuable skills: of recognizing scarcity, of making efficient choices, and of pointing out trade-offs. But it's time to broaden ourselves, to incorporate ecological thinking and ecological values *along with* market thinking and market values—call it, if you wish, "Meadowlark Economics."

I'm ashamed to admit that I took my first elementary class in ecology after teaching economics for more than two decades. I still have a ways to go. I am beginning to read (and appreciate) some of the latter day economists who represent this new thinking: Kenneth Boulding, Hazel Henderson, Herman Daly, Lester Brown, Leopold Kohr, and E.F. Schumacher, to name a few.

In addition, I hope that more and more prominent economists, the Friedmans, Solows, McConnells, the Boskins, Bradys and Greenspans of today—and the future—will feel comfortable not only with traditional market/growth economics, but will also know something of ecology as well; to value the integrity of the environment along with the "bottom line;" to promote development, but *also* protect the standard of living of the other organisms with whom we share the planet.

Along with Environmental Impact Statements (EIS), perhaps future economists can devise what might be called GIS or "Grandchild Impact Statements," making sure our kids and *their* kids will have sustainable quantities of biological as well as other resources, helping preserve our soils and waters, fisheries and forests, whales and bluebirds—even the tiny toads and butterflies—that these entities too will have their voices represented.

So all you National Association of Business Economists, government advisers (and we teachers too), let's dedicate ourselves to a new standard of—what?—Meadowlark Economics if you will, of protecting and sustaining, for the future, a larger and more comprehensive set of durable values.

/ A COMPENSATORY ETHIC

*One of the penalties of an ecological education is that one lives
alone in a world of wounds.*[2]

—Aldo Leopold

ome forty-four years ago, ecologist Aldo
Leopold wove various observations together
into a memorable idea that he would eventually call "the land ethic."[3] To Leopold's
credit his land ethic concept has, over the
years, become a centerpiece vision for ecologists, preser-
vationists, and outdoors people alike. Indeed, I've seen no
better "definition" of so-called Meadowlark Values than can
be found in his book *A Sand County Almanac* with special
attention to his final "Land Ethic" essay. In this essay,
Leopold asserts that we are "members of a community of

interdependent parts and that it's now time to enlarge the boundaries of that community to include not just humans but also plants, animals, soils, lakes, rivers, and oceans, or collectively: the land."

Recognition of this broader community carries with it a commitment of peaceful coexistence with, and protection of, all these diverse natural entities. Summing up, Leopold asks us all to begin changing the role of *homo sapiens* from "conqueror of the land community to plain member or citizen of it."

"Plain member...." I love the word "plain," a word which implies an uncharacteristic dose of humility and modesty. And as we move away from the role of "conqueror," we will begin to see the need for honestly sharing resources, both national and global. Sharing in turn would imply an eventual alteration of our industrial-based standard of living. In this vision, Aldo Leopold has perhaps *begun* to describe an ultimate goal of our species—a true transformation, on a large and permanent scale, of our public and private commitment toward nature. It is a goal that even Professor Leopold realized would take generations to accomplish.

In the meantime, though, what can be done? Are there any intermediate, ethical stances we can use as stepping-stones along the way? Let me suggest one: *a compensatory ethic.*

Compensatory is defined as: "to make up for or to offset; counterbalance; to make equivalent or satisfactory reparation to...." A compensatory ethic would be less revolutionary and in many ways more accepting of the status quo than the land ethic. It would not, for example, insist that we radically curtail our standard of living or necessarily shun many of the pleasures of consumption.

COMPENSATORY INVESTMENTS AND ACTIVITIES

It does, however, imply that if we wish to continue with our resource-using habits, we should somehow compensate or mitigate the damage via investments or activities that will offset the negative consequences of our current level of production and consumption.

An illustration of compensatory ethical action was a decision by a relatively small electrical utility—Applied Energy Services of Arlington, Virginia—to help finance the planting of fifty million trees in Guatemala.[4] This investment is apparently an attempt to compensate for the utility's annual carbon dioxide emissions by planting future carbon dioxide absorbers. Along the same line, I wonder why tropical rainforest countries have not yet made the following compensatory proposal to the developed countries: "Okay industrial friends, if you want our forest diversity and also want to continue to enjoy the fruits of fossil fuels—but don't want the possible greenhouse consequences—you might want to rent our forest of CO_2 absorbers and rich habitats." One candidate for raising money to pay this rent would be a CO_2 user-tax imposed on processes that burn fossil fuels. In addition, this subsidy could (and should) be used to foster the economic survival of tropical populations who would otherwise be slashing and burning tracts of trees to exploit that elusive and short-lived two or three inches of forest topsoil.

If one accepts this line of argument, and begins to explore compensatory ethical options, a number of approaches may pop into mind. The other day, for example, I passed by the site of a new K-Mart. Its enormous parking lot (then empty of cars) looked like a miniature blackened desert. Later I paced the lot's perimeter and found it to be roughly 134 by 143 yards or approximately 19,000 square yards; it was a sizable area with no visible soils or animals—not even a weed!

With such a "sealing of the land," our compensatory ethic cries out for K-Mart and its car-habituated customers (including myself) to make amends for its suffocating surface. Couldn't the company help buy or arrange to preserve a natural habitat—a rare forest grove, a remnant prairie, or a marshland perhaps? Or how about a compensatory contribution to the Nature Conservancy, a group that has demonstrated expertise at this kind of thing?

It would be but a modest investment that would simply reflect "habitat gained for habitat lost." If voluntary contributions are not forthcoming, perhaps a "paving" tax would be in order to subsidize the protection or reclamation of environmentally sensitive areas. Personally, I would feel much better about patronizing K-Mart, Wal-Mart or any shopping center if I were assured that they (we) had paid our dues to nature.

Compensatory ethics is a topic that's challenging to think about and fun to discuss with others. Creativity plus a little ecological understanding is all that's needed to spin out a variety of compensatory strategies. Consider, for example, the ecological implications of deciding to have a child! How then would one apply compensatory ethics to such a decision?

On a simpler level, let me ask you the question: do you burn wood? Our family does. I now hereby pledge to plant as many trees (or more) than we burn each year. This is just common sense and really not much of a burden. I'm surprised how blind we've been to this ethic in our twenty years of burning wood to keep warm. Furthermore, I will try to compensate in other ways. Eventually we may opt for a simpler, less consumptive lifestyle and thereby reduce our compensatory debt.

So all you leaders of business and other readers out there—what are *your* compensatory commitments? If we can somehow make headway with this and other ethical stepping-stones while wending our way toward Aldo Leopold's Land Ethic, then our home planet Earth, so pained and pummeled over the years, would (if it could) spin with "relief," as if knowing we were doing our best to preserve its astonishing aliveness, innate diversity, talent, and ever-surprising beauty.

/ Craftsmanship and Salvation

or some years now, I have had a running argument with my father. It is his opinion that we all move forward by enlarging our individual and collective productivity. He tells me that we must grow two blades of grass where only one grew before. Efficiency and productivity have not only given us our present high standard of living, but they will also be the driving forces for a better future. What are the tools that will bring this about? "More capital investment and better technology" is his answer.

I have always felt that though his position was logically correct, there was yet something intuitively wrong with the argument, but I was never quite able to put my finger on it. After all, isn't it better to drive into town than to walk? And why am I using a typewriter instead of pen and ink? My intuition went awry when I actually observed my own actions.

CRAFTSMANSHIP FOSTERS REVERENCE

But now I think I know what has been troubling me all these years. It is simply this: modern machinery, technology, and the "cult of efficiency" have destroyed craftsmanship. When I speak of craftsmanship, I am not refering to the common complaint today that many of our products are shoddy and poorly designed, though this is to some degree true. Craftsmanship involves more than that. Craftsmanship, to my mind, implies primarily a particular *attitude* toward the shaping of raw materials, and the final product, I think, is only a derivative of that attitude.

Though outwardly inefficient, inwardly the craftsman gains a deep satisfaction through a reverence for raw materials and tools skillfully used. W.H. Auden once wrote that if a person came to him and said, "I have important things to say," he or she would not likely become a poet. But if they said: "I feel like hanging around words, listening to what they say," then Auden felt that this person had a chance.[5]

The craftsman in glass savors glass and the true furniture craftsman loves his wood. It's much like a love affair in which the craftsman ultimately gives birth to some fine work or artifact. Sometimes the process is sensuous and, at other times, the craftsman becomes so totally absorbed that the "self" is forgotten for a moment. It is something like a child intensively concentrating on play; at other times it may be more like a spiritual experience.

Indeed, most craftsmen whom I have known feel that there is a definite "sanctuary" quality to their work. Read, for example, Robert Pirsig's description of tuning a motorcycle:

> *The first tappet is right on, no adjustment required, so I move on to the next...I always feel like I'm in church when I do this...The gauge is some kind of religious icon and I'm performing a holy rite with it.*[6]

Elsewhere in Pirsig's book, he implies that motorcycle maintenance can be an art which can lead to "Zen," an experience where all existence is focused upon the moment, where the pain of the past and the anxieties of the future are dissolved as the worker becomes one with the work.

ETERNAL WORTH VS. TRANSIENT VALUE

Now consider your friends and relatives. How many true craftsmen do you know? Why are there so few? Indeed, why hasn't modern technology given us a broad margin of leisure to pursue these crafts? Though I certainly don't know all the reasons, I do know that when we make an *obsession* out of efficiency and technology, we are likely to diminish our respect for any process that appears to be "inefficient." Furthermore, our high standard of living has given us so many choices that we seem compelled to "consume" each and every variety of experience that is available to us. "Efficient use of time" is the order of the day.

And yet, deep down, I suspect that many of us regret the loss of craftsmanship. I feel confident in saying this because I observe that many people respond with genuine awe when they see a piece of work that comes from the hands of a true craftsman, such as handmade furniture, blown glass, a beautiful quilt, or even a well-crafted poem. We read with envy and respect about the Foxfire craftsmen of Appalachia, preservers of blacksmithing, herbal gathering, stone masonry, and other crafts. We know that somewhere, sometime, we too would like to return to this world of relaxed pace, of deliberateness, and of carefully created forms that reflect what Pirsig called "Quality."

Perhaps what we are really seeking is a kind of salvation. In the final chapter of *Walden* Henry Thoreau implies that a true craftsperson will, in fact, never die! Our technocrats and ministers of efficiency would do well to remember Thoreau's account of the Kouroo artist who strove for perfection in the carving of a walking staff.

After many years of working on the staff with endless love, patience, and complete absorption, he found that "his singleness of purpose and resolution...endowed him...with perennial youth." His friends died, dynasties came and went, and even the polestar changed position! And then at last, when he finally finished his staff, it "suddenly expanded before the eyes of the astonished artist into the fairest of all creations of Brahma:"

> *He had made a new system in making a staff, a world with full and fair proportions in which, though the old cities and dynasties had passed away and fairer and more glorious ones had taken their places, the material was pure, and his art was pure. How could the result be other than wonderful?* [7]

PART II

/ WORK, LEISURE, AND LIFE

/ Less Dependent Workers

nemployment is perhaps the most tragic of capitalism's recurrent economic problems. Idle workers not only diminish the quantity of potential goods and services, but as we all know, unemployment can also be a protracted nightmare for those afflicted. Part of our fear of unemployment is due to the fact that we are exposed to *an unnatural dependency* upon the larger economy and that our livelihood, no matter how competent we may be, is no longer within our control. Economists, with all their theories and proposals, seem to have no reliable solution to the problem. The best they can come up with is to push for policies that promote national growth via macroeconomic measures, a solution that is as remote from the personal lives and personal power of the unemployed as was the original cause of their suffering.

It was while thinking about unemployment in these terms that I came across a couple of interesting readings which started me thinking about the possibility of *microeconomic* approaches to temporary unemployment. The first was from Norman Ware's 1959 book, *The Industrial Worker 1840-1860*. In the introduction, Professor Ware makes a surprising observation concerning the psychic security of the early American industrial worker, before the advent of the monolithic factory system. Ware explains:

> *To the worker, the security of his tenure seemed greater under the older conditions of production, largely because the tenure of the mechanic and artisan was less dependent upon a single function than was the operative who succeeded him. This is seen most clearly in the case of the Lynn shoemakers who in the early years were able to weather repeated depressions in their trade because they were more than shoemakers. They were citizens of a semi-rural community. Each had his own garden, a pig, and a cow...The more highly industrialized this community became, the more completely the worker was divorced from these subsidiary sources of livelihood, the more unemployment became a specter where it had once had some of the characteristics of a vacation.[8]*

And later, Ware amplifies his point again:

> *Before the appearance of the greatly dreaded permanent factory populations, bad times had few terrors for the mill operatives. They simply returned to the farms from which they came, welcoming the holiday, and suffering no ill effects from unemployment....[9]*

One might pause a minute to ponder Ware's surprising conclusions that before the advent of the large-scale factory system, unemployment had "some of the same characteristics of a vacation," or that a layoff was often "welcomed like a holiday."

ELIMINATING THE PSYCHOLOGICAL DAMAGE OF UNEMPLOYMENT

We cannot help but contrast this easy-going, independent lifestyle with unemployment today which can, perhaps, be categorized as a form of psychological violence. On this point, I am reminded of Professor M. Harvey Brenner's unemployment studies in which he found that for each one-percent increase in joblessness, we could (statistically) expect approximately 37,000 deaths over the following six years. He includes among his causes of death a statistical increase in cardiovascular disease, suicides, homicides, auto accidents, etc.[9]

Thus it appears that the psychological damage from to-day's involuntary idleness is considerably greater than in the earlier era. One wonders then, is there a lesson here; can today's worker learn from the semi-independent lifestyle of their early nineteenth century counterparts?

Of course, we must be careful in portraying a microeconomic solution to unemployment that involves returning to a self-reliant homestead economy. Yet on the other hand, we cannot entirely dismiss the surprising popularity of do-it-yourselfism in the United States. Consider, for example, the success of magazines such as *The Mother Earth News, Organic Gardening, New Shelter,* and so on. We do seem to be searching for genuine alternatives in production, at least at the home-economy level.

Still it would be inaccurate to characterize the mass of industrial and service labor as potentially falling within this self-sufficiency model; it's simply not that accessible to most urban workers. Is there, then, any other microeconomic alternative to the problem of periodic idleness?

INDEPENDENT PART-TIME BUSINESSES

That question leads me to the second reading of interest, an article entitled "On Their Own," by Meg Cox in the *Wall Street Journal.*[10] In this piece, Ms. Cox explains how a number of International Harvester workers in Ft. Wayne, Indiana, had set up their own small, part-time business. What is, perhaps, so unusual about this situation is that, unlike most large corporations, Harvester apparently did not frown on its employees moonlighting. In fact, one time when an employee complained to a supervisor that "he wasn't getting sufficient satisfaction" from his Harvester job, his boss responded by encouraging him to "get something more interesting going on the side." And judging from Cox's interviews, that's precisely what many did.

Take, for example, thirty-eight-year-old Stan Urbine. When not drafting or designing Harvester parts, Stan and his brother, Greg, were designing and manufacturing specialty parts for race cars. Then there is Daryl Banet who enjoys repairing cars and tractors in his backyard garage. Also mentioned were part-time carpenters, upholsterers, salespersons, and semiprofessional photographers. These "moonlighting entrepreneurs" not only made extra income from their self-directed, part-time businesses, but also made their lives more interesting by these outside activities. And even more important from our perspective, like the Lynn shoemakers of a hundred years ago, their secondary jobs gave them something to fall back on when faced with the inevitable layoff.

Of course, moonlighting is not exactly a new idea. What seems novel about the Harvester situation is the fact that the corporation did not discourage employees from becoming more independent. Whether International Harvester foresaw possible unemployment down the road (which, in fact, did occur), I don't know. But I would assume that the average large employer is not too pleased to learn that their employees are operating alternative businesses on the side.

Yet, who can fail to see that such an arrangement makes for more secure workers? And when the inevitable layoff arrives, chances are that there will be no black despair, no thoughts of suicide among the Stan Urbines or Daryl Banets of the working world.

In addition, there was no reason to believe that the on-the-job productivity of these men was not as good as their Harvester co-workers. We should note, too, that most interviewees indicated a desire to stay on at Harvester despite their self-created opportunities. We will assume that their salary and, perhaps, even more importantly, their fringe benefits, (plus, no doubt, employee camaraderie) gave them sufficient incentive to keep working for the corporation.

CORPORATE ENCOURAGEMENT OF INDEPENDENT PART-TIME VENTURES

What then are the implications of these examples? Judging by the positive experiences described above, one might go so far as to make the following proposal: Why couldn't large corporations not only condone independent economic ventures, but specifically *encourage* them?

Thus, the "model" corporation would offer employees part-time arrangements to start up their own businesses. In addition, the mother firm would provide market research services to survey potentially profitable niches within the local economy. Furthermore, I see no reason why the company could not provide a credit-union or venture-capital bank to help finance the tools or training that might be required to get one's business underway. Such an arrangement may lead to productivity benefits for the farsighted company that initiates such a program, psychic security for the semi-independent employees and, finally, if accomplished on a large scale, economic benefits for the nation.

This is indeed an interesting model to consider. Lately we have been hearing a lot about Japan's system of "life-time employment security." Yet I doubt if the Japanese model is always applicable to the American industrial worker given many workers' proclivity for individualism and independence.

The other arrangement, where the worker has the opportunity to seek out his or her independent niche within the local economy, is, I believe, more realistic and more in tune with our national temperament and historic traditions.

/ An Ideal Boss

Where other companies speak of a supervisor or foreman, IBM speaks of an assistant....He is to be the 'assistant' to his workers. His job is to be sure that they know their work and have tools. He is not their boss.[12]

—Peter Drucker

et's take a moment to examine a very interesting and important question: "What are the qualifications of an ideal boss?" This individual might be one's supervisor in a business, or perhaps in a university or government agency. Since "supervisor" and "boss" have connotations which do not fit the ideal, let's use instead the more appropriate term, *administrator*.

What then should this model administrator do or not do? What are his or her functions within the organization, and how does this person differ from the traditional "bosses" of today? Undoubtedly every business writer has his or her own

29

list of skills and competencies needed to become the so-called "effective manager." For my ideal administrator, however, let me suggest but four. If you allow me to use what many might consider to be an odd metaphor, I'll call the first function:

ADMINISTRATOR-AS-GARDENER

I use this term because gardeners, especially organic gardeners, *see their present activity in terms of the long run.* Like characters in the ancient Chinese proverbs, they look for a payoff far into the future. Good gardeners prepare their soil for years ahead.

They begin gathering materials now in the form of old hay, kitchen scraps, and manure to make compost that may not break down for a year or two. Once the compost is added to the soil, the gardener may not see results until the following year or even after that. With this kind of time perspective, gardeners tend to be optimists in the sense that they are convinced that small decisions today will add considerable quality to the enterprise many years hence.

In addition, gardeners seem to enjoy the art of experimenting, and do not seem to get upset if some new project fails. They are anxious to try new varieties, new ways of planting and irrigating, new ways to build up topsoil—things that add interest and excitement and offer the experimenter something to look forward to.

Now the *administrator-as-gardener* views his or her operating unit in a similar way, with the ultimate goal being the long-term success of the enterprise and the well-being of the workers. The administrator ought to offer encouragement, praise, and opportunities for individual development, knowing that these actions may not have a payoff immediately, but will surely nurture happier, more loyal, and more productive workers for the long run.

The *administrator-as-gardener* also encourages experimentation and expects frequent failure, for this is what makes the job interesting and creates possibilities for true innovation. Indeed, this particular role is the administrator's most satisfying, for it offers the greatest potential for making lasting improvements.

ADMINISTRATOR-AS-INTERVENER

The second function is *administrator-as-intervener*. Of the four, this one comes closest to the conventional "boss." It refers to the fact that the head of a unit must communicate the larger objectives or missions of the organization to the workers. Combined with this duty, he or she also has the responsibility to intervene in those cases in which a worker disregards the goals or the specific policies of the hierarchy.

Judgments must be made quickly when such behavior seems likely to threaten the reputation or effectiveness of the unit. Nothing is more demoralizing to the rank-and-file staff than the times when those outside of the work-unit begin to view the group with diminishing esteem, particularly when the problem lies with one or two individuals. Such menacing behavior is often brought to a halt by one's coworkers. But when that fails, the administrator must intervene or the end result may well be *more control and regimentation imposed by the hierarchy.*

This kind of intervention involves an immense amount of tact, plus an ability to criticize and persuade the individual to change his or her actions, without damaging the worker's sense of self-worth. If the one-to-one intervention does not work, then the administrator must sound out the staff for their suggestions for handling the situation. Perhaps psychiatric help is in order. As a last resort, there may be no choice but to fire the worker. But whatever the solution, the administrator must know how to handle this delicate situation with great diplomacy. *Administrator-as-intervenor* is not an easy job!

RESOURCE PERSON

The third function of our ideal administrator is that of *resource person.* Indeed, this is a function or skill that many conventional supervisors may find most difficult to learn. For a good model of this function, let me suggest one from the medical industry: i.e., the hospital administrator's relationship to the doctors.

A hospital administrator is normally not a "boss," but is seen more *as a servant.* The administrator regards the doctors as professionals *who know best how to do what they are doing.* He or she is hired to take care of administrative details such as the patients' records, billing, etc., details to which the doctors do not have time to attend. A good administrator in this role should, therefore, visit various departments and ask questions like: "What can I do for you?" or "I have certain resources and skills that might make your job easier; how can I be of more help?" Although this approach may sound logical, how often do we hear such helpful words from our supervisors?

The main thing to keep in mind is that the *administrator-as-resource-person* should always regard his or her staff members as experts in their respective fields who, from time to time, will need extra services and resources that only someone in an administrative position can provide. I see no reason why this idea cannot be applied in the executive suites of General Motors, in the administration of a university or government department, or even between worker and foreman on the assembly line.

ADMINISTRATOR-AS-LOBBYIST

The fourth and final function is *administrator-as-lobbyist.* In almost all large organizations, there is competition between departments and divisions for scarce resources. These resources are usually thought of in terms of money and staffing. But they might also include other benefits such as the quality of the workplace, access to policymaking, flexibility, and other tangibles and intangibles that are conferred on the subunits by the hierarchy.

Therefore, it is important that our administrator learn a little of the art of politics and public relations. There will be times when the lobbyist role demands even more than the usual political representation, especially when the survival of the unit is in question. On such occasions, we would want our administrator to know how to fight effectively, and how to battle with skill and determination for recognition and continuance of the unit. He or she must know how to deal with subtle power plays of others who may be out to destroy. In such times, the administrator must convince the hierarchy that his or her unit is not only making short-term contributions to the larger organization, but that it recognizes and is working toward the long-term objectives as well.

Of course, this kind of political activity can be an unpleasant business. The administrator may feel it a necessity to make friends with people they do not particularly like. They may have to "advertise" the unit's virtues and minimize its faults.

Unfortunately, many individuals in this role feel the need to overlook illegalities such as bribes, kickbacks, padded expense accounts; or they may lie about dangerous products, or quietly poison the environment. But to do these things and offer the excuse that the "ends justify the means" would be in strict violation of the other functions. Such unethical actions *will* eventually catch up with the guilty party—first on a personal, moral basis; next with his organization and, finally, publicly. When this happens, he jeopardizes the morale and possibly even the survival of the unit, those things that had taken years to build up as a resource person or gardener. When an administrator engages in such questionable activities, it's essential that the people within the unit act as the intervener; at first, privately, then publicly if necessary.

Nevertheless, the ideal administrator will, at times, be in situations where he or she must be realistic about power relationships within the organization, where they must aggressively defend the unit against encroachments as well as make the necessary compromises that do take place in any political arena.

But if the lobbyist-function is performed well, there can be no better payoff than to have the staff respect their administrator. And it is this simple respect which will ultimately make the other roles of *resource-person, intervener,* and *gardener* that much easier and thus foster the growth and well-being of all concerned.

/ HENRY THOREAU AS ECONOMIC PROPHET

ecently, while reading some of Henry Thoreau's writings, I became more and more convinced that this nineteenth century American is truly an economic prophet for *our* time. Indeed, I am wondering why we have not elevated Thoreau to the ranks of the major historical economic thinkers—not so much the mathematical economists of today but more in the tradition of the great economic philosophers such as Smith, Hume, Marx, Malthus, and Ricardo. Not a British economist, nor a German, but this time one of our own.

THE PROBLEM OF OVERABUNDANCE

Let's begin with the "farm crises" of recent years. Although agriculture has always had its ups and downs, the farmer who overexpanded, acquired too much machinery, too much land, and, in general, incurred too much debt is now facing an especially demoralizing situation in which: (a) he's probably losing money year after year; and (b) he's finding it difficult, if not impossible, to get rid of his holdings. Though Thoreau did not specifically predict this farmer's dilemma, he did make a generic observation that seems wonderfully relevant to the situation. That is, Thoreau constantly warned of *the problem of overabundance,* and that our possessions can, at times, "be more easily acquired than got rid of."[13] In the following passage from *Walden,* change the image slightly and see how Thoreau's vision has a surprisingly contemporary ring to it:

> *How many a poor immortal soul have I met well-nigh crushed and smothered under its load, creeping down the road of life, pushing before it a barn seventy-five feet by forty, its Augean stables never cleansed....*[14]

Whether farms, homes, businesses, or general possessions, Thoreau had great compassion for those who had *too much,* whose overabundance was a drag on their lives.

But if possessions and expensive overhead do not represent "the good life" for Thoreau, what does? Might it come from the advance of technological conveniences? No doubt Henry marveled at, and benefited from, many of the byproducts of the industrial revolution. He admitted to the advantages of shingles, boards, bricks, and especially glass window panes ("doorways of light...like solidified air!")[15] in the construction of homes. And of course, as a part-time surveyor and pencilmaker, he no doubt valued the various tools of these professions; but, for the most part, Thoreau felt that inventions tended to be nothing more than "improved means to an unimproved end"[16] or "pretty toys which distract our attention from serious things."[17] At worst, our technology could be profoundly destructive to life itself. Consider, for example, the following quote:

> ...but though a crowd rushes to the depot, and the conductor shouts 'All Aboard' when the smoke is blown away, and the vapor condensed, it will be perceived that a few are riding, but the rest are run over.[18]

"Run over." A strange statement it seems. But not so out of place when we consider all those who die in transportation accidents. And if Thoreau wrote these words metaphorically (which I believe he did), who cannot recognize the rather chilling prophesy when one considers the dangers of nuclear weapons, a catastrophic leak at a chemical factory, or an atomic power plant going berserk?

Or consider the giant machines that devour hundreds of square miles of landscape in their pursuit of minerals or trees, or to prepare the land for suburban developments and airconditioned shopping malls. "But lo!" Thoreau exclaims, "men have become the tools of their tools."[19]

This kind of economic "progress," i.e., that which ravages the environment, would have been quite distressing to Thoreau as he strongly felt that there simply could not be a "good life," nor even a completely healthy life, without access to Nature:

> How important is a constant intercourse with nature and the contemplation of natural phenomena to the preservation of

*moral and intellectual health. The discipline of the schools or
of business can never impart such serenity to the mind.*[20]

or:

*There can be no very black melancholy to him who lives in the
midst of nature and has his senses still.*[21]

And finally:

*We need the tonic of wildness—to wade sometimes in marshes
where the bittern and the meadow-hen lurk, and hear the
booming of the snipe; to smell the whispering sedge where only
some wilder and more solitary fowl builds her nest, and the
mink crawls with its belly close to the ground.*[22]

WILDNESS AS PRESERVATION OF THE WORLD

So now picture, if you can, this relatively young man (thirty-four) standing before the Concord Lyceum in the spring of 1851, opening his lecture with the statement: "I wish to speak a word for Nature, for absolute freedom and wildness," and ending with the famous phrase: "...in wildness is the preservation of the world."[23]

His audience must have found these very strange words. Strange because of the immense area of pure wilderness still existing on the North American continent at that time. But it's different now. Today it is not nearly so difficult for us to understand what Thoreau was trying to explain to his New England audience over a hundred years ago.

Thus, Henry Thoreau wished we might value our natural environment and work hard to preserve it against the forces of degredation. But what else did Thoreau advocate? What did he recommend individuals do to help themselves in their private economic lives? His answer was as profound as it was brief and emphatic: "Simplify, simplify!"[24] In an exaggerated moment, he advised his readers to "keep your accounts on your thumb-nail."[25]

More realistically, Thoreau advocated that we reduce our economic needs, that is, engage in a sort of "voluntary poverty."[26] His greatest skill, he once remarked, "has been to want but little."[27] Another prophetic notion? Perhaps so, especially when we consider that, sooner or later, the industrialized countries will be forced to a lifestyle which requires less use of energy and natural resources.

REEXAMINING OUR BASIC OBJECTIVES

In addition, if Thoreau were alive today, he would probably be appalled by our tremendous private and public debt. He would also be upset over our growing dependence on government and the myriad of specialists who reduce our capability for doing things ourselves. He would be pushing for greater individual economic independence, as much as was practical. He once suggested that we might learn to grow our own food as well as build our own homes.

And indeed, if we actually were more self-reliant, as our Concord economist suggests, wouldn't inflation lose some of its sting, the threat of recession lose much of its terror? Wouldn't our feverish anxiety over economic growth diminish? And, in general, wouldn't life itself be more pleasant if we could slow down and become a little less serious in our striving for high material comfort? Thoreau honestly felt that with some modest readjustment in our expectations, we might view man's existence in a much different and more positive light:

> *In short, I am convinced, both by faith and experience, that to maintain one's self on this earth is not a hardship but a pastime, if we will live simply and wisely....*[28]

In conclusion, Thoreau, as economic-philosopher, is asking us to reexamine our basic objectives. He is telling us that our traditional goal of high material consumption may well carry with it an unexpected price tag in the form of unpleasant complexities and anxieties.

Thoreau's main goal would thus be freedom; or better yet, what he simply called *life.* "The cost of a thing is the amount of what I will call life which is required to be exchanged for it immediately or in the long run."[29]

For many contemporary economists and business people, this is indeed an odd theory of value, but it is one that Henry Thoreau would defend both in his writings and in the way he lived his own life. It is an economic principle that would force us all to look at our own individual lives *and* the larger economy in a different perspective: not GNP per-capita, but something more like "life per-capita," if that could somehow be measured.

Thoreau was genuinely concerned for the economic welfare of his fellow man, but he did not want us to waste our life pursuing overabundance. He profoundly wished that we might enjoy our years within the larger living universe, maturing and ever growing, and *not* wake up one morning, late in life, to discover we had never really lived.

PART III

/ ECONOMIC FORECASTS,
FUTURES, AND PHILOSOPHIES

/ Consensus Forecasting—A Ten-Year Report Card

ow accurate are economic forecasters? This is not only an interesting question, but an important one too. Why?

First, reliable predictions imply that our macroeconomic models are relatively valid. This would be good news for those who have spent their professional lives investigating the ins and outs of the complex and intricate phenomenon we call the U.S. economy.

One might also argue that accurate forecasting will help make economic decisionmaking more efficient—whether it is government's projecting future revenues and expenditures, or profit-seeking businesses utilizing forecasts to make informed investment decisions. Indeed, one might argue that high-quality forecasts (if taken seriously) might even

contribute to smoothing out the age-old business cycle.
Surely these are good reasons to hope for long-term forecasting accuracy.

Consensus Forecasting

To answer the opening question, "How good are the forecasters?" let's look at the ten-year record compiled by the
Sedona, Arizona-based forecasting newsletter, *Blue Chip
Economic Indicators*. *Blue Chip* calculates averages from the
forecasts of approximately fifty nationally known economists.
Each month, editor Bob Eggert calls his cooperators and
asks them to give projections for major economic variables
such as real gross national product, inflation, and so on.
These figures are then averaged. This forces, in a sense, a
"consensus" among the fifty economists. *Blue Chip* has been
compiling forecasts for a decade now and thus offers a
unique opportunity to highlight some of its successes and
note some of its shortcomings as well.

Real GNP Growth

To begin, it appears that Blue Chip's most striking success
(I'm giving it a "B+" grade) is its ten-year record in predicting the growth of real GNP on a year-to-year basis (see Figure 1 and Table 1). For example, the average error for *Blue
Chip's* October forecasts—made for the following year—was
only one percentage point. In other words, we would expect
Blue Chip's October average to be no greater than one
percentage point above or below what the actual real GNP
growth rate turns out as reported by the Commerce Department's Bureau of Economic Analysis (BEA) some fifteen

months later. Figure 1 shows the close alignment of *Blue Chip's* October forecasts compared with actual (except for the surprise recession year of 1982).

Figure 1

10-Year History of

Blue Chip Consensus Forecasts of Year-over-Year

Percentage Changes in Real GNP vs. BEA Actuals

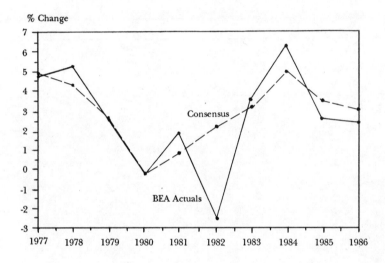

Of course, *Blue Chip* continued its surveys after October and as expected, their error dwindled somewhat as they begin projecting GNP growth into the "current" year (see Figure 2). For example, the average error for forecasts made in February is only nine-tenths of a percentage point; by April it is down to six-tenths.

Blue Chip Economic Indicators also makes quarterly GNP forecasts. Here, however, the record is not nearly so impressive. As a teacher, I would assign them a "D" grade and add a reminder note—"Needs improvement!" In fact, due to the great volatility of quarterly GNP changes, we found an astonishing degree of inaccuracy of *Blue Chip* forecasts—even when the group tried to predict what was going on during the *current* quarter. Obviously, we might expect an error something less than the year-to-year error of one percentage point.

Table 1

Blue Chip vs. Simplistic Trend Method
A Comparison in Forecasting Accuracy
for Percentage Change in Real GNP

Forecast for	Blue Chip consensus forecast[1]	Simplistic trend forecast[2]	BEA actual	Percentage point forecast accuracy of Blue Chip	Percentage point forecast accuracy trend method
1977	4.9	4.9	4.7	+0.2	+0.2
1978	4.3	4.7	5.3	-1.0	-0.6
1979	2.7	5.3	2.5	+0.2	+2.8
1980	-0.2	2.5	-0.2	0.0	+2.7
1981	0.9	-0.2	1.9	-1.0	-2.1
1982	2.2	1.9	-2.5	+4.7	+4.4
1983	3.2	-2.5	3.6	-0.4	-6.1
1984	5.1	3.6	6.4	-1.3	-2.8
1985	3.5	6.4	2.7	+0.8	+3.7
1986	3.1	2.7	2.5	+0.6	+0.2
				1.0	2.6

10-Year Average Accuracy (in percentage points)

[1]Forecast for the year indicated as published in prior October issues of *Blue Chip Economic Indicators* (full year over prior year).

[2]Simplistic Trend Method assumes the current year will be the same as the previous year (final actual).

In actual fact, the error in current quarter predictions turned out to be well over twice as much as the year-to-year error. And strangely, the error did not seem to change much as the panel looked ahead to two quarters, three quarters, etc. Herein lies a "red flag" warning for the media when they insist on asking their all too frequent question: "Can you give us the projected growth rate for the current as well as the next three upcoming quarters?" They should realize that whatever the answer, on the average the error will be between 2.6 and 3.2 percentage points!

Figure 2
10-Year History of
Average Monthly Percentage Point Error in
Blue Chip Consensus Forecasts vs. BEA Actuals

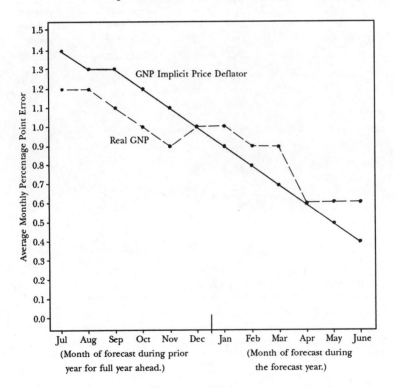

Out of curiosity, I then asked myself: "How accurate would we have been if we had used what might be called "the simplistic trend method forecasting?" The trend method would assume that the "current" quarter will be the same as the "previous" quarter. Although the *Blue Chip* error was high, the simplistic trend error was slightly higher—averaging 3.4 percentage points as compared to *Blue Chip's* 2.6 error.

Table 2

Blue Chip vs. Simplistic Trend Method
A Comparison in Forecasting Accuracy
for Percentage Change in GNP Price Deflator

Forecast for	Blue Chip consensus forecast[1]	Simplistic trend forecast[2]	BEA actual	Percentage point forecast accuracy of Blue Chip	Percentage point forecast accuracy trend method
1977	5.6	6.4	6.7	-1.1	0.3
1978	6.0	6.7	7.3	-1.3	-0.6
1979	7.3	7.3	8.9	-1.6	-1.6
1980	8.5	8.9	9.0	-0.5	-0.1
1981	9.1	9.0	9.7	-0.6	-0.7
1982	7.8	9.7	6.4	+1.4	+3.3
1983	5.7	6.4	3.9	+1.8	+2.5
1984	5.0	3.9	3.8	+1.2	+0.1
1985	4.7	3.8	3.3	+1.4	+0.5
1986	3.8	3.3	2.7	+1.1	+0.6
				1.2	1.0

10-Year Average Accuracy (in percentage points)

[1]Forecast for the year indicated as published in prior October issues of *Blue Chip Economic Indicators* (full year over prior year).

[2]Simplistic Trend Method assumes the current year will be the same as the previous year (final actual).

Incidentally, running the same simplistic trend method for the year-to-year real GNP projection (assuming that "next" year will be the same as "this" year), the trend method gave an error 2.6 percentage points—making even more impressive *Blue Chip's* earlier mentioned average error of one percentage point (see Table 1).

Forecasting Inflation

Perhaps the second most important indicator for an economy is its inflation rate; and arguably the best measure of inflation is the GNP implicit price deflator, as this figure takes into account price changes in all sectors of the economy.

Again using the benchmark forecast month of October (of the previous year), *Blue Chip's* ten-year average error for the deflator was 1.2 percentage points. Note that this figure is not quite as good as the accuracy figure for real GNP growth. Even more discouraging for the *Blue Chip* economists was the result obtained using the simplistic trend method (see Table 2). Note that the trend forecast produced an average error of only one percentage point for predicting inflation. Indeed, this surprise revelation apparently put some "egg on the faces" of some of our nation's top forecasters.

There is, however, a brighter side to the inflation report card that can be seen in Figure 3. When the past decade's inflation rate is graphed, we see a steep, pointed "hill," indicating that inflation rose rapidly (from 6.7 percent in 1977 to 9.7 percent in 1981) while after that, the rate of inflation moved down to a low of 2.7 percent (1986). Plotting *Blue Chip's* October projections against the actual inflation rates, we see *Blue Chip's* averages following "actual" up at a near equidistance, like hunting dogs taking after a wily fox. At the top, the fox makes a sharp turn and heads

Figure 3

10-Year History of

Blue Chip Consensus Forecasts of Year-over-Year

Percentage Changes in the GNP Implicit Price

Deflator vs. BEA Actuals

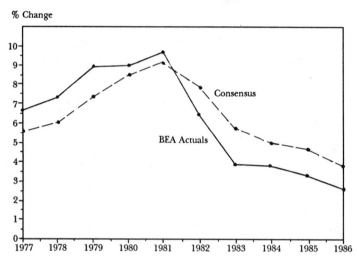

downhill; the determined dogs also make the turn, but stay approximately the same distance behind their prey. In other words, the *Blue Chip* forecasters get the direction right, but—out of a collective *disbelief* that inflation could move up so fast, then down even faster—they missed their objective by roughly the same amount both on the way up and on the way down. Now if some kindly poet-oracle had whispered to each of the forecasters the following advice:

> Inflation rate up?
> Add one percent
> For forecasting fame.
> Inflation rate down?
> Subtract the same!

they would have nearly "caught the fox." The error would not have been 1.2 percentage points, but something less than four-tenths of a percentage point.

And finally, let's look at *Blue Chip's* inflation forecast over time. Although *Blue Chip's* October error merits something like a "C" grade, the error diminished impressively as the months went by. For example, by the time the June calls came in, the average error was only four-tenths of a percentage point.

All things considered, *Blue Chip's* consensus report card for the past ten years shows neither an embarrassing nor a poor performance. In fact, much of it is quite good, though there will always be room for improvement—especially in the category of quarterly forecasts.

Not bad, *Blue Chip*. But let's see if your report card can be even better ten years from now, after your second decade of consensus forecasting.

/ PRO-GROWTH VS. ANTI-GROWTH

any of those in the forecasting profession, whether working for private business or for government, are very likely pro-growth economists. There are, however, a number of maverick economists and other writers whose voices over the years have become a little stronger, a little firmer, who are actually questioning the prevailing ethic that continuous growth is desirable, particularly for the United States and other industrialized countries (the "overdeveloped nations," as Leopold Kohr calls them). All of these writers are concerned with what they see as negative results of economic growth: the steady erosion of the quality of the global environment and the decline or degradation of the world's nonrenewable resource base. Perhaps the extreme point of view comes from Ezra Mishan of The London School of Economics:

55

You could very well have stopped growing after the First World War. There was enough technology to make life quite pleasant. Cities weren't overgrown. People weren't too avaricious. You hadn't really ruined the environment as you have now.[30]

Let's now take a brief look at *both* positions beginning with the prevailing view, i.e. defenders of economic growth who tend to accept Adam Smith's historic contention that "the progressive state is in reality the cheerful and the hearty state to all order of society. The stationary is dull; the declining melancholy."[31]

PRO-GROWTH ADVOCATES

There is the view among pro-growth advocates that humans are surprisingly *adaptable* and that our species has proven over thousands of years that it is capable of making appropriate change when change is warranted. If we run low on certain resources, our market economy (through higher prices) will signal that it's time to find (or create) new substitutes: fiber optics instead of copper, strong (and inexpensive) plastics in place of steel or aluminum; or perhaps a trend toward miniaturization to conserve a myriad of scarce resources. If fossil-fuel supplies become depleted, we will (pro-growth economists say) find substitutes or evolve more highly efficient systems with our technological know-how. In this sense, the pro-growth position seems to go hand-in-hand with what we might call "technological optimism."

And we should pause to consider Irving Kristol's argument that growth is, in fact, *a necessary precondition* to a modern democracy in which "the expectations of tomorrow's bigger pie, from which everyone will receive a larger slice,...prevent people from fighting to the bitter end over the division of today's pie."[32] Defenders of economic growth also point out that very few families can say that they are satisfied with their current economic status. In addition, they remind us that we still have many lower-income people in the United States who are likely to be permanently poor in a zero-growth economy. A final point from pro-growth economists is that it is much easier to deal with pollution in a growing economy; cleaning up the environment will be expensive, and the additional resources must come from somewhere.

Defenders of economic growth are greatly disturbed that an increasing number of people want to go back to the "good old days"—days that pro-growth people believe were not so good. They ask, "Why can't environmentalists and other anti-growth advocates understand that technology and economic growth are conquering nature for the benefit of mankind?"

Author Mel Ellis, a naturalist who has demonstrated unique sensitivity for both economic and environmental problems, writes

> *Man almost literally made the cow, the fat corn kernel, the plump turkey, the beautiful rose. And if he erred in his enthusiasm and polluted his raw materials, his resources, he still made the world enormously better.*[33]

ANTI-GROWTH ADVOCATES

Most environmental advocates probably do understand the benefits of technology, progress, and economic growth, but their attention is directed to different concerns. They are listening to different sounds. Essayist E. B. White once summed up this attitude with the comment,

> *I would feel more optimistic about a bright future for man if he spent less time proving that he can outwit Nature and more time tasting her sweetness and respecting her seniority.*[34]

The immediate concerns of environmentalists are not the eradication of poverty or the benefits of high-speed air travel or the advantages of the computer over the abacus. They do not see a thousand acres of timber as so many completed homes. They see the grandeur of the forest and its enduring value as a generator of oxygen, a climatic stabilizer, and a habitat for plants and wildlife—and they work for its preservation. Instead of seeing the Appalachian hills as a source of strip-mined coal for heating homes, they ask, "What are the adverse consequences of strip mining for the land and its inhabitants?"

> *The D-9 bulldozer is the largest built by the Caterpillar Tractor Corporation. It weighs some 48 tons and is priced at $108,000. With a blade that weighs 5000 pounds, rising five feet and curved like some monstrous scimitar, it shears away not only soil and trees but a thousand other things—grapevines, briars, ferns, toadstools, wild garlic, plantain, dandelions, moss, a colony of pink lady-slippers, fragmented slate, an ancient plow point, a nest of squeaking field mice—and sends them hurtling down the slope, an avalanche of the organic and the inorganic, the living and the dead. The larger trees that stand in the path of the bulldozer—persimmons, walnuts, mulberries, oaks, and butternut—meet the same fate. Toppled, they are crushed and buried in the tide of rubble.*[35]

Along the same line, who could not empathize with the novelist James Michener's feelings of sadness and guilt after he returned to the site of his boyhood stream?

This marvelous stream in which I used to fish and where as a boy I had gone swimming, this ribbon of cool water which has been a delight to generations of farmers, was now a fetid body of yellowish water with not a living thing in it. Frogs, fish, waterlilies, bullrushes, and ducks' nests had all vanished...The loss of my stream had occurred under my nose, as it were, and with me making no protest. When I finally saw what had happened, I was ashamed of my inattention. What in those years had I been doing that was more important than saving a stream? If we continue to abuse and destroy our resources, many of us will be asking that question thirty years from now, but by then it will be too late, and some of the precious things we have lost will not be recoverable.[36]

Environmentalists, in short, are distressed by the ugliness of overdevelopment. They are angered by worldwide pollution in such forms as oil spills and acid rain and also by the growing lists of extinct or endangered species of animals and plants. They feel that these are the unnecessary consequences of human selfishness. They are saddened by our blindness—a blindness to the possibility that much of what we value today may be lost forever. Of those who favor "development at any cost," they ask, "Why can't you see what uninhibited growth is doing to those things we must preserve for future generations?" The great debate over growth is based on simple but profound differences in values. It will, undoubtedly, remain a public issue of great magnitude for years to come.

/ The Coming Repair Age

ave you ever broken your glasses? No, not the lens, but that thin plastic section in the middle of the frame? Surely it happens to people now and then, for it recently happened to me. Now if your frames did break, did you try to repair them? Were you successful?

My broken glasses got me to thinking about the importance of mending skills, particularly in relation to our present and future economic situation. After considering the matter for a while, I came to the conclusion that we really ought to be putting more of our energies into the art of repair and maintenance.

It's no secret that the world's energy supplies will someday dwindle, and that our once large supply of raw materials will become more scarce. Simple arithmetic tells us that there must, someday, be an end to wastefulness. In short, most intelligent people know that we will not be able to continue our gross consuming habits for the long run. Therefore, there seem to be but two fundamental choices. The first is simply "more of the same," i.e., continued rapid growth and an inevitable collapse. The second choice is to move toward a *repair society*, one that sustains itself largely on what we have today with, perhaps, a number of new and worthwhile inventions from time to time.

I hope we select the second alternative, the one where we consciously *choose* to save those things that seem to offer us the greatest usefulness, and then keep them in sound working order for ourselves and for posterity. This mode of living begins with a basic appreciation for the elegance of repair and the ritual of maintenance.

I began to reach this conclusion while reading a lovely little book, entitled *Craftsmen Of Necessity*, by Christopher Williams. Consider the following quote from Mr. William's book:

> *The indigenous societies of the world gear their lives to a small assortment of deeply loved goods, gently made, carefully used and lovingly repaired.*[37]

When I first read this passage, I was reminded of a little African stool that I once came across. There is no doubt that this lovely artifact with its circular, concave seat and gay, though somewhat distorted, faces on each of its three legs, was the work of a true craftsperson. But of greatest interest to me and what brought the most admiration was its exquisite repair work.

Small pieces of broken wood were sewn together with thin copper wire, the ends of which were artfully coiled in concentric patterns that contrasted wonderfully with the dark stain of the smooth wood. Where parts had to be bridged, there were short, flat lengths of copper scrap tightly bound to the broken pieces. Magnificent!

Imagine someone taking an interest in preserving this useful artifact over the years. One might even speculate that these handsome repairs were made over a much longer period of time, perhaps a hundred years or more; I don't know.

I do know, however, that the Gurungs (a tribal community of central Nepal) have shown equal ingenuity and a repairer's reputation may well span generations:

> *The Gurung's compulsive resourcefulness is almost an embarrassment to the casual observer. Axes, ploughs, and digging tools are used until they are worn beyond recognition. The village blacksmiths then reincarnate the stubs into another generation of tools and utensils; Aama can recall the lineage of successive incarnations of each of her pots, ladles, and hoes....*[38]

AMERICAN RESOURCEFULNESS

Do the above descriptions of ingenious improvisations, artful repair, and meticulous maintenance describe *our* future? I believe they do, even though surely we have a ways to go to match their art and skill of mending and maintenance. Yet, putting artfulness aside, there may be some of us who are not too far behind when it comes to equaling their ingenuity. I think of a farmer who lives down the road. Here is a man who, years ago, became quite annoyed when successive pickup trucks began to rust and then deteriorate. He noticed, however, that where oil had collected onto areas of the truck or other machinery, the machine's parts remained rust-free and workable. Or if the old oil was protecting paint, the enamel underneath was as shiny and colorful as the day he bought the machine.

The obvious conclusion was: If only he could find a way to saturate all rustable areas of the truck with oil, he could keep it working well, perhaps, forever! My friend thus had to find a method to spray oil into the furthest reaches of the truck's framework. He would also need to coat the insides of doors, rocker-panels, fender seams, the hollow of the tailgate, all the bolts, springs, nuts, and screws. Through trial and error, he finally developed a remarkably efficient spraying device out of a junked oil-filter canister from a twenty-five-year-old Chevy; a simple improvisation which could deliver vaporized oil to all points in and around the truck. He had to drill appropriate holes and do other ingenious things to get a correct amount of air and oil together. He then snapped this contraption onto his air compressor, attached a long hose with a tiny thumb-press nozzle, and he "was in business."

My friend once asked me to examine carefully his sixteen-year-old Ford truck to see if I could find any rust breaking through. I looked and looked and looked. There was none. Believe me, I was impressed. And he accomplished this feat with discarded junk and waste oil. My friend now has a truck which, with infrequent oilings, he should be able to pass on to another generation—a Gurung at heart!

Another neighbor of mine has successfully nursed along a thirty-year-old Allis Chalmers hay-baler. He knows everything about it. Everything. And he can make virtually any repair without fear or befuddlement.

These are just a few examples of the harbingers of a new maintenance ethic, prophets of "the coming repair age." For the rest of us...well, we will just have to develop our repair skills by trial and error mixed with some advice, now and then.

Incidently, I did surprise myself when I finally fixed my broken eyeglass frame with one of those new "super glues," but it's not particularly elegant. Nothing like the mending of the stool.

No, most of us have a ways to go to learn and practice this art of repair and maintenance so prevalent in traditional societies. It will surely be something new for us, we who are so accustomed to the wasteful ways of mass consumption. Or, we might look at the future repair age as simply "coming home again," safely, after the big party. With luck, we just might make it.

PART IV

/ PERSONAL FREEDOMS,
GLOBAL RESPONSIBILITIES

/ Freedom To Build

hile walking the streets of New York, or rambling about Washington, D.C., one first becomes aware, then astonished, and finally depressed to see so many homeless. Actually some of these street dwellers do have "homes": a cardboard box here, a grate-heated improvisational lean-to there, a cave-like structure under plastic only a few feet from busy passersby. Others have nothing.

As I consider this situation, I sometimes think back to my Peace Corps days in rural Kenya in the mid-1960s. I honestly cannot recall seeing any homeless at all despite the obvious poverty prevalent in all corners of the African countryside. What goes on here? How could this be?

I suspect that part of the answer is that the Kenyan situation had benefited from obligations within the tribal culture including the protective role of the extended family. But equally important is the fact that it's relatively *easy* to construct shelter in rural Kenya. People have access to raw materials, often nothing more than poles, mud, and thatch, but also ingenious use of log slabs, tin roofing, plywood, chicken wire, reinforced concrete and other available materials. My own impressions were that these simple dwellings were dry, relatively comfortable and, by Kenyan standards, roomy. Some homes were not only resourcefully built, but were also quite innovative in design and use of space.

BUILDING CODES AS OBSTACLES

In contrast, here in the United States, there are numerous obstacles to self construction. This is particularly true if you want to build something less than "standard" housing (usually defined by middle-class values), but above (many notches above) the flimsy impromptu street shelters. I am therefore wondering why we can't learn from our Kenyan friends by providing some kind of niche for those who want the freedom to build—to designate suitable places, to create opportunities, and to establish a nonintimidating climate and friendly infrastructure so average people with or without capital can contribute something to satisfying their housing needs. Isn't this the spirit and the hands-on reality of Habitat for Humanity, a program that has gone a long way to dispel stereotypes about poor people and their ability to provide "sweat-equity" for simple, but solidly built housing?

Some twenty years ago, my wife and I built (and still live in) a small yet comfortable home using inexpensive pole-construction techniques outlined in an unconventional building book entitled *Your Engineered House.*[39] In no other single area of our lives did we learn so many useful things. We discovered that construction forces you into an objective pragmatism—you see what works and what doesn't; and in the failures and successes, you began to understand an innate truth concerning materials and processes: "Everything that happens," wrote Marcus Aurelius,

happens as it should and if you observe carefully, you will find this to be so.[40]

Call it "reality training," call it "empowerment," or see it simply as the satisfaction of knowing that you are contributing to a basic need, something we humans have done for ourselves since Ice Age times.

Indeed, housing-poor city dwellers may easily have the intelligence, strength, even the time, money, or credit, but are stymied by regulations, bureaucreatic red-tape, and rigid building codes which have erased most, if not all, the low-cost options. Whether affecting the poor or nonpoor, the frustrated renter or the totally homeless, it's disheartening to see well-meaning regulations (designed to help protect unwary buyers from unscrupulous contractors) inhibit people *from even thinking about* constructing their own shelter.

SOCIETY SHOULD PROVIDE ADVICE AND ASSISTANCE

Society should not discourage owner/builders, but instead *encourage* them. To improve the climate for building freedom, we should allow for owner/builder amendments that would modify the rigid codes and the coercive city building inspection system while maintaining practical standards for sanitation, structural stability, and fire prevention. For specified areas, democratically elected zoning commissions would not be out of line to prevent totally unregulated shanty-towns from developing. Having met the sanitation and safety requirements, the emphasis should then turn to do-it-yourself and community-based building freedom.

As a positive approach, why can't we use the building inspector not as "Big Brother," but more *as a voluntary resource*, something along the lines of a County Agricultural Extension Agent? As you probably know, the county "Ag" agent is the person you call when you have questions about your farm operation. He or she is armed with inexpensive government publications packed with information based on up-to-date research and professional advice. If need be, the agent will come out (at no charge) and check corn blight, soil quality, feeding problems, or some other aspect of his operation where help is requested.

In a similar way, why couldn't there be a "City Building Agent" (former inspector) who would offer the same kind of courteous and expert services to individuals or families interested in home construction? The County Extension Service has been an immensely successful program, indeed a popular program since 1914. Is there any reason we could not apply the same principle to housing as well as other community needs? Unfortunately it seems difficult for politicians to understand that light-years of difference separate the coercive system of the code-inspector from a system of voluntary expert-as-a-resource.

MAN'S UNIQUE EVOLUTIONARY SPIRIT

Of course well-meaning laws that have the effect of inhibiting freedom and innovation are not new. They can be traced at least as far back as the secretive guilds and the stagnation of the Middle Ages. Yet, whenever we use coercion to

regulate those private areas of endeavor, it not only dimin-
ishes our potential, but in some ways I believe violates a
unique evolutionary spirit—a spirit that needs wide latitude
to learn and yes, even to make mistakes.

In a broader biological perspective, I think Lewis Thomas
was right when he observed that our ability to explore and
even "blunder" is the real marvel of our uniqueness.

> *We are at our human finest, dancing with our minds, when
> there are more choices than two. Sometimes there are ten, even
> twenty different ways to go...and the richness of selection in
> such a situation can lift us onto totally new ground. This pro-
> cess is called exploration and is based on human fallibility. If
> we had only a single center in our brains, capable of respond-
> ing only when a correct decision was made, instead of the jum-
> ble of different, credulous, easily conned clusters of neurones
> that provide for being flung off into blind alleys, up trees,
> down dead ends, out into blue sky, along wrong turnings,
> around bends, we could only stay the way we are today, stuck
> fast. The lower animals do not have this splendid freedom.
> They are limited, most of them, to absolute infallibility...*[41]

In conclusion, I believe that we should value and preserve
those freedoms that allow us to explore and to learn,
freedom to meet our needs and enjoy our successes too—in
short, freedom to proceed at widely different angles!
Wherever you happen to live or whatever your economic
circumstances, providing shelter is surely one of those
freedoms.

/ SOME LIBERAL PRAISE
FOR MILTON FRIEDMAN

ccasionally one of my economics students will ask: "What do you think of Milton Friedman?" conservative economist and Nobel Laureate in economics. My answer?

Although I continue to have some ideological disagreements with the man, (more on this later) I confess he has changed my mind on a variety of topics—more times than I really care to admit. Sometimes Friedman takes me by surprise, insisting (with his unforgettable smile) that I focus my scattered liberal views into a focal plane that highlights the twin values of economic freedom and efficiency. On other occasions, he gathers his notions, stuffs them into my pocket while I carry them around (sometimes for years), plucking them out every so often, thinking about them and, to my astonishment, finding my initial disagreements fading away.

FIRST CONTACT WITH FRIEDMAN'S IDEAS

My first contact with Friedman's writing came at the end of my undergraduate years at a small liberal arts college. The Econ staff tended to be of liberal persuasion and, to their credit, required all economics majors to read Friedman's *Capitalism And Freedom*[42] for our comprehensive exams.

I carefully studied this little green paperback and dutifully marked it up with a dull pencil. As I page through the book now, I note the many question marks, not dainty notations of polite disagreement, but heavy, angular marks as if I were angry with the author or, more accurately, with his ideas. His views seemed to contradict much that I thought was correct. My liberal inclinations said that government intervention in economic affairs was both necessary and good—from fiscal policy's countercyclical measures to the welfare state to the public school system. Friedman, on the other hand, was telling his readers that such intervention is, more often than not, destructive to individual freedom, to the efficiencies of the economy, and ultimately, to our standard of living.

At that time, I could not agree with him. Indeed, the large question marks remained in my little green book for some years. Yet, even in these undergraduate years, I was impressed with Friedman's ability to communicate. I discovered a warmth to his writing and an unusual respect for his nonprofessional readers. He generally shunned much of the "distancing jargon" of economists. For example, the term we like to describe generalized pollution costs is "externalities," whereas Friedman devised a softer, more easily understood metaphor of "neighborhood effects." Other Friedman metaphors and phrases that I have heard over the years, now stick in my mind like lines from a childhood poem; the following, for example, is fun to dramatize in class, amplifying the word SHOUT, while muting down *(pianissimo)* the word "whisper":

Special interest groups speak with a shout, while the public at large speaks with a whisper.

Well, it's been over two decades since I read *Capitalism and Freedom*. And although Friedman has not made me a true conservative, I do respect many of his insights and arguments.

In addition to his little green book, I recall reading, in the intervening years, *Newsweek* magazines that frequently featured his essays. By the time I got to the business section, I was often weary of reading. But there, smiling face and all, was "Uncle Milt" with some more unsettling ideas. "Now what's on his mind today?" I asked myself.

In one issue, Friedman is upset with teenage unemployment. Indeed, nonwhites face unemployment rates something over thirty percent. Cynically, I wondered if a conservative was really sensitive to this issue. "We liberals are the sensitive ones," I say to his smiling face. And what's Friedman's solution? Eliminate the minimum wage to open up entry level jobs. Although my first reaction was quite negative, I came to accept the fact that if a government-imposed wage is above a particular labor market's equilibrium, then there will tend to be surplus labor (unemployment) as employers cut back their hiring as workers simply become too expensive. In addition, Friedman would point out an interesting ethical consideration: what right does the government have to interfere with a willing seller of labor (at an agreed-upon wage) with a willing buyer? If nothing else, Friedman forced me to think hard about the issue of occupational freedom.

Also, Friedman's observations on price controls of natural gas, again using the principles of supply and demand were, in retrospect, quite correct. He pointed out that a price ceiling (imposed price below equilibrium) would discourage production and encourage wasteful consumption. Today, we've deregulated natural gas and most economists would agree that it was the right thing to do. Another related issue is city rent controls (or price ceilings) which again discourages construction of rental properties and encourages more potential buyers at the controlled price or rent level. The result? Shortages! For economics teachers who readily teach the tools of supply and demand, Friedman reminds us that we should take these principles seriously, by applying them to real-world issues and acknowledge the serious problems when there is governmental interference.

OTHER FRIEDMAN THEMES

But there is more. I recall reading in the green book Friedman's suggestion of a "Voucher System" for financing public schools. The idea was relatively simple: local governments would offer parents twelve years (per child) worth of "portable grants" so that they could *choose* the kind of education that dovetails with the child's abilities, proclivities, and values. It would be something like a "GI Bill of Rights" for school-age kids. According to Friedman, such a system would have the effect of off-setting the present public school monopoly making K-12 schooling more competitive, more accountable, and very likely more innovative.

There are now, of course, experiments in "School Choice" around the nation as politicians and the public grapple with new ways to confront a deteriorating educational system. If the voucher system, or something like it, proves to be successful, we would all have to give Milton Friedman a good deal of credit for introducing the idea thirty or so years ago.

Another early Friedman idea was "the Negative Income Tax" (NIT). This program was designed to replace our current income-transfer system including AFDC, Food Stamps, public housing, and so forth. The negative income tax would give families or individuals a portion of their "unused exemptions and deductions" if their incomes happened to fall below the poverty line—a simple, logical idea which would efficiently offer everyone in need a guaranteed minimum income. Actually, Friedman's negative income tax was not a difficult idea for me to accept. I don't think it is too much of an exaggeration to say that most economists, liberal and conservative, favor some form of NIT over our present welfare system, a system that has been characterized as both inefficient and destructive to family life.

Incidentally, all these ideas and proposals have been made above and beyond Friedman's contributions in the scholarly field. Here, his monetary theories have gained wide acceptance throughout the profession. In short, Friedman says that "money matters" in relation to stabilizing the business cycle (whereas in the Keynesian model, the key consideration is the overall level of spending). Although Friedman's recommendation of "increasing the money supply at a relatively constant (3 to 5 percent) rate has not been universally accepted, his emphasis on the general *importance of money* is respected in the economics profession.

Friedman's research and theories of monetary policy undoubtedly played a major role in the decision to grant him the Nobel Prize in economic science. Thus, most economists feel that here, in the field of monetary history and monetary policy, lies his greatest contribution.

But I'm not so sure. Indeed, I am tempted to place Friedman's legacy with his NIT or voucher system or, perhaps, with his instructive use of simple supply and demand to help establish free market policies. I am tempted to say that these ideas are his greatest contributions. But no. There is something more.

FRIEDMAN'S IDEAS ON LICENSURE

His idea of greatest importance just may be the little-discussed observation already mentioned in *Capitalism and Freedom*. It is one of those ideas next to which I had placed a large question mark many years ago but am now taking much more seriously. What is it? What will Friedman perhaps be remembered for a hundred years from now? It may be his observation concerning the destructiveness of certification and licensure. Picture, if you will, Milton Friedman standing before a large gathering of the American Medical Association (AMA) (which he did) and saying, in effect, "One of the major problems facing American medicine is the fact that doctors are licensed."

He would go on to tell them that licensure has the effect of reducing the quality of medical care (a) by reducing the number of doctors, (b) by requirements that make medical professionals too high-priced, (c) by making it difficult or impossible for paramedics or other kinds of practitioners (such as midwives) to enter the industry, and finally, (d) by discouraging wide-ranging alternatives to the standard AMA-type medical practice. Incidently, each of these arguments had already been meticulously defended in his green book. Each possible objection, Friedman anticipated and carefully answered.

I must confess that Friedman's exposé of the AMA as a vested-interest group, or worse yet, a *union*, pleased me greatly. "An act of courage," I thought to myself.

But the issue of licensing doesn't stop with medicine. Friedman also went on to discuss the detrimental effects of licensure in relation to all licensed professions—from pharmacists to librarians, from teachers to stockyard commission agents. In each case, the potential negative impact of licensing is the same: licensing erects barriers to free entry, it restricts free choice, and often raises the price to the consumer.

For each, the professional society, or union, sets up obstacles in the form of credentials. If, for example, they wish to improve compensation, they have the option of erecting even greater barriers to entry, barriers in the form of additional schooling, longer apprenticeships, etc. Friedman also pointed out that these techniques do not always guarantee high-quality professional services. In some cases, prior requirements may have little relationship to the task that will eventually be performed. Or we might find that with some professional groups, such as doctors or college professors, there is often no retesting of performance after the initial examinations. Furthermore, anyone who comes to the job qualified but not licensed, or anyone who has a new way of solving problems cannot, by law, practice unless he or she goes through the long and arduous education-certification-licensing process.

Has Friedman got something here? I, for one, think he does. But to the best of my knowledge, few people have studied this problem very seriously. One writer who has realized that something is amiss in the world of credentials is Ivan Illich. Illich's attack on contemporary education with his rallying cry for "deschooling society" has made him one of the more interesting iconoclastic philosophers in print.

In his book *Deschooling Society*, Illich points out that educational competence can and should come in all sorts of packages. He also observes that the generally accepted system that insists upon narrowly defined credentials is not only harmful in U.S. schools, but is, perhaps, even more disruptive in Third World countries.

In short, Illich believes in "competence," but feels it ought to be detached from educational credentials.

Inquiries into a man's learning history must be made taboo, like inquiries into his political affiliation, church attendance, lineage, sex habits, or his racial background.[43]

Ivan Illich, like Friedman, has also made some harsh comments about the modern medical monopoly in his book *Medical Nemesis*. Illich seems angrier (his language is definitely more politically charged) and yet, I believe he is saying some of the same things Friedman—and perhaps even Friedman's mentor Adam Smith—said many years before.

If you allow me to digress for a moment, I'd like to share with you a daydream I had recently. I was picturing a lecture delivered by the great Scot himself. The year? 1776. In the front row, sitting together, were Mr. Illich and Mr. Friedman, while from the upper balcony I saw the two men apparently quite excited and nodding in mutual agreement as Professor Smith quoted from his new book, *Wealth of Nations*:

> *The patrimony of a poor man lies in the strength and in the dexterity of his hands; and to hinder him from employing this strength and dexterity in what manner he thinks proper without injury to his neighbor is a plain violation of this most sacred property. It is a manifest encroachment upon the just liberty both of the workman and of those who might be disposed to employ him. As it hinders the one from working at what he thinks proper, so it hinders the others from employing when they think proper. To judge whether he is fit to be employed may surely be trusted to the discretion of the employers whose interest it so much concerns.*[44]

I'm now wondering about intellectual traditions and how some students take worthwhile ideas from their mentors, polish them and present them clearly to a new age. These students perform a valuable service. Therefore, from this writer at least, some genuine liberal praise for our own Nobel Laureate and champion of choice, Dr. Milton Friedman.

OF SUSTAINABLE FUTURES AND "SEEING DEEPLY"

"So, now where do you *disagree* with the guy," students ask? If you have been reading the preceding essays, you have probably detected a new direction of thought, a modulation of values if you will, away from today's free market *drift* based on individualism and material acquisitiveness, toward a future whose local, national, and global economy embraces ecological integrity and resource sustainability. The evolution of human society toward that goal may need intelligent guiding, convincing, nudging—engaged leadership if you will—to divert that drift from steady environmental degradation toward healing. I doubt if Friedman's pure free market orientation will, on its own, instigate these changes (although market approaches and the business form of organization may certainly help once the direction and incentives are in place). So where does this "guiding and nudging" begin?

I'm not exactly sure, but I do recall a helpful suggestion by environmental activist David Brower. He said that much of our future economic growth and job creation could be in a context that emphasizes ecological and environmental *restoration*. One might also add the importance of *cultural* restoration as well. And like drops before a gentle rain, we *are* beginning to see humble examples here and there. Consider the following comments by an urban observer, Marcia Lowe, on recent civic developments in Portland, Oregon:

> *Its vibrant downtown boasts such green spaces as Tom McCall Waterfront Park, once an expressway, and Pioneer Courthouse Square, formally a parking lot.*[45]

In addition, Lowe praises the land-use planners of Curitiba Brazil, a model of what could be taking place most anywhere in the world:

> *A former gunpowder/munitions storage was turned into a theatre; an old glue factory is now a community center....*[46]

Often environmental restoration comes about through public demand and financing, or as discussed earlier, private individuals and businesses can participate in various ways including a commitment in the form of a "compensatory ethic" (see pages 9-12). In addition, *any* pollution control (or pollution avoidance) technologies, or firms that contribute to energy efficiency, recycling, or cost-effective renewable energy, will assist (indirectly at least), in environmental restoration. Again, these new directions may take political or community initiatives to get underway, a friendly, democratic "Visible Hand" one might say to those admirers of Adam Smith. But once the ground-rules have been set, consider the myriad possibilities for new businesses, skills, and jobs!

Even on the personal level, I'm wondering if the Friedman/Smith economic self-interest model is really appropriate as we distance ourselves from the Industrial Revolution and move into what WorldWatch Director Lester Brown calls an "Environmental Revolution."[47] Wouldn't this revolution, to some degree, imply a new ethic of behavior, a new level of awareness and perhaps a new definition of what is *truly* our self interest? If so, who are those we might turn to for guidance in this postindustrial future, who might now be our mentors?

Perhaps one of them is really an old acquaintance—Henry David Thoreau—a person who's been standing in the wings, waiting for us to listen to his message on natural wonder and economic simplicity (see pages 35-40). Indeed, the personal component may not be so much a political "Vision," but simply a new way "of seeing" or "of looking deeply," as the Buddhist monk Thich Nhat Hanh once wrote.

In a recent book, Nhat Hanh suggests that we take time to "look deeply" at a piece of paper. What do you see? Perhaps you will "see" the tree that was cut down and transported to make the paper (do you see evidence of deforestation?). Can you see the sunshine, topsoil, and rain that sustained the tree? How about the logger (and *his* needs)? What about soil run-off, or chemical pollution? Can you see nonhuman creatures who are affected by economic processes? In our current economic mode, Nhat Hanh seems to be saying (in contrast to the free market model) that we actually enjoy very little liberty:

> *We are imprisoned in our small selves, thinking only of the comfortable conditions for this small self, while we destroy our large self.*[48]

At the beginning of this piece, students were asking me about Milton Friedman; now in our postindustrial, postmaterialistic era, I have a question for them: "Are you ready to start *your* work, to begin listening, connecting, and *seeing* ever more deeply?

/ Growth and Global Pollution

he air you breathe may seem clean to you. Of course in some notorious metropolitan areas, such as Los Angeles, Mexico City, Lagos (Nigeria) and Krakow (Poland) there is more often than not, a disagreeable smog which we know causes respiratory and other well-documented health problems. But even in small towns and villages, you will find air pollutants derived from a variety of sources. In one test of air quality, biologists look for the presence or absence of lichens—the lovely, colorful, scale-like growths that cling to rocks and trees in noncity environments. But the sensitivity of lichens to even low levels of air pollution makes them a rare sight in populated areas. Even more subtle, invisible air contaminants are, unfortunately, becoming more and more prevalent *no matter where on earth measurements are made.*

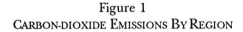

Figure 1
CARBON-DIOXIDE EMISSIONS BY REGION

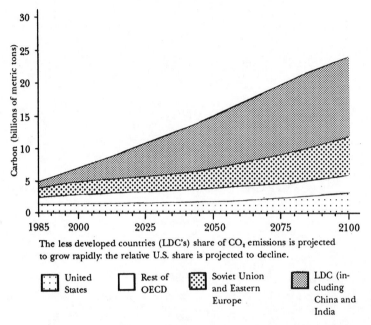

The less developed countries (LDC's) share of CO_2 emissions is projected to grow rapidly: the relative U.S. share is projected to decline.

United States   Rest of OECD   Soviet Union and Eastern Europe   LDC (including China and India)

Traces of synthetic chemicals plus carbon and sulfur dioxide (both byproducts of fossil-fuel combustion) are intermixing throughout the global atmosphere. These emissions are mainly the result of human activities connected with industrialization and economic development. Indeed, the *Economic Report of the President* (1990) expresses great concern about the levels of current and projected future emissions; its conclusion makes no pretense that the solution to reducing these gases will be a simple one. In one chart (Figure 1), the *Report* indicates that the greatest increases in carbon dioxide (CO_2) between the years 2000 and 2100 will be in Third World countries.

For example, consider China—a country that currently has the largest coal reserves in the world and plans to *double* its coal consumption by the end of the 1990s!

Yet, even without *any* additional CO_2 releases, we know that since the Industrial Revolution, economic activity has already increased the concentration of this gas by roughly 25 percent (from 280 parts per million [ppm] to approximately 360 ppm).[49] The result is the very real possibility of global warming, or the so-called "greenhouse effect." Setting aside for a moment the honest differences of climatologists as to whether warming has already begun, author Bill McKibben, in his book *The End Of Nature*, asks us to pause and reflect on the fact that we have *already* altered the earth's atmosphere:

> *Most discussions of the greenhouse gases rush immediately to their future consequences—is the sea going to rise?—without pausing to let the simple fact of what has already happened sink in. The air around us, even where it is clean, and smells like spring, and is filled with birds, is different, significantly changed.*[50]

EARTH'S ALTERED ATMOSPHERE

Global warming, according to theorists, begins with an increase in carbon dioxide and other greenhouse gases, such as methane, chlorofluorocarbons (CFCs), and nitrous oxide. The altered atmosphere then traps *additional heat*, which in time increases oceanic evaporation and, hence, atmospheric water vapor. Water vapor, in turn, is an efficient greenhouse gas itself and invites further warming in a "looping" feedback process that may be difficult to reverse. Possible increases in average temperature range between a conservative 2°F and a relatively large 8°F. Temperatures in the higher range would probably be great enough to begin to melt the polar ice caps. Along with such projections, some scientists argue that the earth may have some positive, self-regulative abilities, such as the absorption of excessive CO_2 by the oceans or the possible formation of protective cumulus-type cloud covers.

Thus, like a football player subjected to continual bumping, bending, and bruising, the earth is also under stresses initiated by human activities and technologies and fueled by economic development. What we don't know is whether the earth's "body" can absorb these physical insults, and like a young, well-conditioned athlete demonstrate resiliency, bouncing back without injury when the stress lets up.

Or is our planet more like a middle-aged, weekend player, whose nasty bruise to the knee or shoulder may be more or less permanently disabling. Environmental pessimists, looking at the ominous trends of future pollution, might remind us that even the most resilient athlete who experiences repeated traumas can be permanently injured and face severely diminished health and life processes. The precise metaphor is currently unclear, but its configuration in relation to climatic change will probably come into focus within the next ten to fifty years.

Other concerns related to developmental activity include the ongoing destruction of tropical rain forests. When a tract of forest is cut and burned to accommodate cattle ranches or small farms or to harvest tropical woods, it compounds the greenhouse effect by reducing plant photosynthesis, which absorbs CO_2, and by releasing additional CO_2 into the atmosphere when wood is burned. It is estimated that rainforest destruction contributes roughly 20 percent of the CO_2 buildup that climatologists have been measuring in recent decades.

Another concern related to the destruction of tropical rain forests is the *extinction of entire animal and plant species*. In addition to their intrinsic ecological value, the disappearance of biological diversity also has serious economic and potential health implications for human beings:

> *The fact that many medicines contain active ingredients obtained from substances in plants and animals, especially those in the tropics, suggests that a reduction in diversity could represent a significant economic loss.*[51]

Peter Raven, Director of the Missouri Botanical Garden, estimates that approximately one-fifth of all plant and animal organisms are "at risk" of becoming extinct during the next thirty years.[52]

A further complication of rainforest loss combined with climatic change is the possibility of extreme weather events. Indeed, James Lovelock, originator of the *Gaia theory* (which regards the planet as a self-regulating system that behaves as if it were a living organism) feels that the increased frequency of violent weather—superhurricanes, tornadoes, tidal waves, and record high and low temperatures—ought to be one of our main concerns:

> *The destruction of the tropical rainforests and the greenhouse effect are so serious—they're not just the doom stories of scientists.... They will come in the form of surprises: storms of vastly greater severity than anything we've ever experienced before.*[53]

Ozone depletion and acid rain are further destructive side effects of worldwide atmospheric pollution. But in these areas there may be greater possibilities for clean-up through the use of alternative technologies for coal-fired burning (the major cause of acid rain) or substitutes for known ozone-damaging chemicals (such as chlorofluorocarbons).

In summation, world development has produced—and probably will continue to produce—problematic environmental side effects, the most serious of which could have an adverse impact on the earth's climatic balance. Many economists point out that additional research is needed and that the costs (especially before all the relevant data is in) may simply be too high, given the uncertainties. Consider, for example, all the individual workers and industry-energy related businesses (including coal mining, electric utilities, automobile manufacturers, ore and metal companies, and airlines, to name a few) that would be adversely affected by a sudden or even a slow shift away from oil and coal usage.

Erring on the Side of Caution

Other economists say that we had better not wait: if we err, we should, as the saying goes, "err on the side of caution." Rushworth M. Kidder addresses this issue in his essay "Let's Not Wait for 'Proof' on Warning of Global Warming," when he argues that we should not evaluate clean-up costs based on certainties; instead, we should view them as costs or premiums paid on a global health-insurance policy:

> We need to change our metaphor. We need to stop looking at environmental issues as though they were court cases. We need, instead, to think of ourselves as homeowners buying insurance. You don't insure against the absolutely predictable. You protect against the possible...You defend yourself against large and irreversible damages.[54]

In fact, some progress has already been made within the developed countries. The United States has initiated a reforestation plan, and some electric utilities have committed company resources to planting trees. In addition, Sweden has taken the important first step of levying a CO_2 emissions tax.

Also, in the Montreal Protocol—a twenty-four-nation treaty signed in 1987—the representative countries pledged to reduce ozone-depleting CFC emissions by 50 percent by the year 2000. Although the directive was strengthened in 1990, new evidence of ozone thinning, and even possible ozone "holes" over North America, accelerated the schedule of CFC production phase-out by 1995 or before. Indeed, many environmental groups see the Montreal Protocol as a model for future negotiations that will address even more complex environmental problems, such as atmospheric warming, on an international scale.

Economists are beginning to rethink developmental strategies for the Third World countries that are compatible *both* with planetary health and with the betterment of living standards for the world's poorest nations. Working out such short- and long-term policies will be the great challenge of the coming decade and the early part of the next century. Given the complexity of these issues, economists would be well-served not only to have a grounding in politics (the traditional science of political economy) but also to synthesize their discipline with ecology as well.

For government officials, this same approach is equally valuable. Considering the enormous implications of today's decisions for tomorrow's generation and the next—in both the developed and the developing worlds—our leaders might well heed the advice of Lao Tzu, written in the fourth century B.C. Toward the end of his little book, *The Way Of Life*, dedicated in part to helping the ruling class of his era, Lao Tsu writes:

> *Solve the small problem before it becomes big.*
> *The most involved fact in the world*
> *Could have been faced when it was simple*
> *The biggest problem in the world*
> *Could have been solved when it was small.*[55]

When we consider human impact, world economics, global population, and the environment, such advice is as solid, wise, and true today as ever.

PART V

/ LEARNING FOR ALL AGES

/ Topsoil Drama

...the care of the earth is our most ancient and most worthy and, after all, our most pleasing responsibility. To cherish what remains of it, and to foster its renewal, is our only legitimate hope.

—Wendell Berry

opsoil, we know, is an essential resource to maintain life on this planet. However, building topsoil is a slow, slow process—and losing it can be dishearteningly swift. Surely these are important facts for all of us to know, and perhaps especially important to impress upon young people.

With these thoughts in mind, I felt that a "natural history of soils" might be a useful, and even fun topic when my wife asked me to do a project for her Girl Scout day camp. Starting with a suggestion from Del Thomas, a local soil scientist, we decided to do the unit in the form of a play or drama. In addition, we tried to make the drama relatively simple so that others might try it (or some variation of it) with a minimum of cost and preparation. Here is an account of what we did.

We gathered twenty girls, aged seven to twelve, for a one-hour activity. I began by suggesting they pick up some topsoil and asked, "How important is this in keeping you alive?" This question created an excellent opportunity for all of us to think through the essential nature of what we commonly refer to as "dirt." Of course, all our vegetables, our fruit and our grains are directly dependent upon soil. But other food such as meat and dairy products, are *indirectly* dependent upon it as well.

How about a pizza? How do the ingredients directly or indirectly depend upon topsoil? What about lumber for our homes, paper for books and writing, cotton and wool to keep us warm? What about butterflies and bumblebees, foxes and birds? Yes, all of us depend upon a food chain (or more accurately, a food pyramid) which begins with this grey/black crumbly substance under our feet.

How Soil is Created

Next questions: "Where does soil come from?" Here I brought out a jar of water with a tablespoon of alum mixed in. (The alum, which can be purchased at a grocery store, helps separate the various soil components.)

We then put a handful of our collected soil into the water, screwed the lid on tightly and let everyone give the jar a shake. Within a minute it became obvious that our soil had at least three components: first the small stones and sand that remained on the bottom; next, the silty or fine clay particles of the middle, and finally, the decomposed vegetable matter floating on top. Having observed this, I asked the girls if they would like to be in a play in which we could "make" some soil.

"Yes," they shouted unanimously, "yes."

"OK, let's begin at the beginning—that is, with rock (probably from a volcano) which, over time, breaks up by wind and water. Which of you wants to be a volcano?" (Many hands shot up.) I chose a volunteer and placed a pre-prepared volcano sign around her neck. From my son's rock collection, I brought along a sample of volcanic rock—i.e., a hand-sized piece of light-weight pumice. We passed it around, then gave it back to the girl designated "Volcano."

"Anyone want to be water?" I got a couple of volunteers and gave them "Water" signs. "Now who wants to be wind?"

I explained that wind and water "will act as these elements did approximately a billion or so years ago—that is, break up the volcanic rock into smaller and smaller pieces of sand and stone." Since we were talking about long time periods, I pointed out that these sand particles were carried about (mainly by water) and eventually came to rest. There they sat. And with more and more sand coming in on top of the sand, the layers and layers became tightly packed together, as if they were cemented or glued.

This newer, compressed rock we called Bedrock Sandstone. (In our area, we have many outcroppings of Paleozoic sandstones dating back about five hundred million years.) I showed the girls a piece of local sandstone and asked, "Who wants to play the part of Bedrock?" I chose six or seven "Bedrocks," put signs on them, and asked these girls to huddle together on the ground. I then explained, "When we start the play, Wind and Water will 'wave' and 'blow' through Bedrock, breaking it back into individual, 'unglued' sand particles."

Adding to the fun, I asked someone to be "Glacier." (Here in western Wisconsin, glaciers came through a number of times in the last two million years, ripping up the bedrock, grinding the pieces down, and carrying this soil-making material to our area. Some of the sand in our jar, I pointed out, may easily have come from hundreds of miles north of us.) Thus, Glacier, in our little drama, had the job of "crunching and grinding" and moving Bedrock sand particles even more.

The remaining girls, except one, were given the signs for "Plants." As Plants, they would "grow and die, grow and die" (i.e., fall on the ground, wriggle up, fall down, wriggle up, again and again).

At this point, we briefly returned to the jar of water and soil. I showed Plants that they would "become" the floating, decayed matter on top, while the finer particles would be in the middle, and the broken-up Bedrock would end up as sand on the bottom.

The remaining girl played "Mother Time." Her job was to hold her hands up and "hover" over all the activity. The drama now began. And what a scene it was! Volcano's pumice was tossed aloft again and again. Wind and Water broke up Bedrock while Glacier crunched and jostled about and moved Bedrock girls even more. Meanwhile, Plants grew and died, grew and died, at a steady pace. After a few minutes, I asked them to "stop" and to try and appreciate how much actual time must take place to make soil.

"Once bedrock is broken up, it takes approximately five hundred years to make one inch of topsoil!"

"Let's pretend that ten seconds is one hundred years of time. Everyone freeze and consider all the things that are happening. Mother Time will hold her hands over the scene, and I'll call out every one hundred years (that is, every ten seconds). Remember, nobody can move—you must simply think about everything going on."

"One hundred years...two hundred years...three hundred years..." (Frozen kids. Each ten seconds seemed unbearably long.) "Four hundred years...(and finally) five hundred years."

"And after all this work, here is what we have...Ta Da..." I pulled a towel off a pie pan and on the bottom was one inch of preprepared soil. It was a grand achievement.

"But," I asked, "is it enough to grow a tree?"

"No."

"Could it grow a stalk of corn?"

"No."

"Perhaps a small seedling at best. We'll obviously have to make many, many inches to grow a tree."

While we were discussing this last point, a gust of wind (fortuitously) came through, creating an opportunity to demonstrate wind erosion. I picked up some soil from the pan and let it blow out of my hands. Another handful (I blew on it this time), and that soil was gone, too.

I was now beginning to sense an element of frustration, even some anger at what I was doing. All that work! All that time put into making our inch of topsoil, and how easily and quickly it had been blown away by the wind. We looked down at the pan. It was a depressing sight...spots of bare, polished aluminum. Now we couldn't even grow a small seedling.

I then took the girls to a worn path that went down a bank to a creek. The trail was bare of vegetation and had begun to show signs of erosion. Question: "Why is the path losing its soil?"

We noted that the vegetation, which contributes to the making of soil, is also important to keep it from washing away, especially on a steep slope. I then put some topsoil on the path and asked the girls where they thought it would eventually end up after the first hard rain.

It would obviously be carried down into the creek. We then mentally followed its inevitable trip to our local Red Cedar River, to the Chippewa River, and the Mississippi River, and finally into the Gulf of Mexico. (Here it would have been helpful to bring along a map of the United States) Now, standing streamside in our concluding moments, I once again asked the girls to remain quiet for a moment and think about everything we had learned in the past hour.

The long geological and biological processes of soil-building plus the depressing feeling of losing it—these were the things that I wanted the girls to know and also to *feel.* Indeed, it's an experience that we all should have from time to time. And from this knowledge, we will hopefully become more respectful and more vigilant in preserving the soil we still have—a resource so amazing, so precious, and as we witnessed this day, so very vulnerable, too.

/ A PASSION FOR LEARNING

believe the purpose of teaching can be stated quite simply: teaching ought to instill a *passion for learning*. That is, if teachers are doing their job, they will be helping their students acquire a lifelong love for learning. The end product is long-run rather than short-run as students grow and mature until the end of their days. If teachers don't somehow move their students toward this objective (even in a small way) I don't think they can be considered successful.

Deep down, I have a feeling that success should not be too difficult. Indeed, the process of growing and becoming a more self-reliant learner, of prospecting for humankind's creations and discoveries, ought to be an exciting adventure full of delights and surprises that touch both heart and mind. Yet as we all know, this is often not the case. Teachers with enthusiasm and the best of intentions frequently end up as mechanical dispensers of information and facts. Many feel that the only way they can overcome the student's resistance to learning is to "force-feed" them, through the use of various instruments of power and fear.

Power and fear! These seem to be the tools most frequently used "to get the job done." What a frustrating situation this must be for a new teacher with high hopes and good intentions. And from the viewpoint of the students who recall the fun of learning new things on their own before schooling, and who wish to become persons of greater value later on in their lives, the situation is even worse. Such students must feel robbed. What was once an inner-directed drive for learning has now become *motivation-based upon trying to please other people* so that one can successfully "get through the system." For those who eventually want to become self-learners, the work of undoing the damage is very difficult, if not impossible. It's as if one were to try to decontaminate radioactive substances. Is there any hope for this unfortunate state of affairs? Under our current schooling system, the prospects appear dim. And yet it is interesting to note the few cases in which these suffocating results did not occur. For example, among the various teachers I have known, there have been a few who apparently have been able to avoid these pitfalls. They did not succumb to the usual mechanical teaching. Instead, they retained their enthusiasm year after year; and what is even more important, they succeeded in instilling in their students a genuine excitement for learning. What was their secret? What qualities did these memorable teachers have in common?

THREE CHARACTERISTICS OF SOME SUCCESSFUL TEACHERS

From my observations, they all had displayed the following three characteristics: First, these teachers put a high priority on creating *a positive attitude* toward their subject matter, as opposed to the usual goal of simply "imparting a certain body of knowledge." It's not that information and facts are unimportant, but they should be used more as a vehicle to excite students about the process of learning. Students will crowd around after "the bell," eager for more, opening up to suggestions for new areas of exploration, and even making new connections on their own. When these things happen, the teacher will know they are on the right track.

The second ability is *to tie other areas of knowledge into their own discipline*, then relate this material to the student's own experiences and current level of knowledge. This quality implies that the teacher is interested in diverse subjects and thus is a *good model for self-learning*. I believe students often feel a certain "disconnectedness" as they travel from one little box of knowledge to another. The sum often becomes *less* than the disconnected parts. And unfortunately the students rarely develop skills that will help them tie these seemingly disconnected parts together. When the integration is done expertly as with a Carl Sagan, a Loren Eisley, or a Lewis Thomas, the performance can be breathtaking! Yet there seems to be no attempt in our schools, from kindergarten to graduate school, to cultivate these integrative skills or reward teachers who pursue them. In fact, it's more often the case that those who have the most advanced schooling and therefore are the most specialized, become our future teachers. They, in turn, tend to raise high the walls around their classes.

But now let us assume that we can avoid the problem of overspecialization. Also assume that we are able to retain an unusual degree of enthusiasm. And yet, we still find our students unhappy and resentful. It's a situation in which things ought to be OK; but, instead, we find resistance to change and growth, and we realize that we have not awakened in the students their potential for learning. What's wrong? What have we missed?

This brings us to the third and, perhaps, most difficult quality to attain, for it involves some decontamination on the part of the teachers themselves. The third quality that good teachers have is a high regard for the student. Actually, it's even more than that: they all demonstrated a *profound respect* for their student's innate intelligence and potential for discovery, and treat it at least as equivalent to their own. This means that a teacher of physics, for example, would give the *same respect*, the same esteem, to their own students that he or she would give to "the heroes" of their discipline: i.e., as if a young Isaac Newton or Marie Curie were sitting in.

For many teachers, this third quality involves a radical rethinking of what education is all about. Indeed, we find no simple techniques that will help the teachers out on this one. But when respect is there, it is really there; *the students know it!* It is transmitted in a thousand little ways. It operates like a magic whirlpool which loosens the muscles of resistance and thaws cold fear. It's no longer merely a power relationship, but a relationship among equals. When a student says something impressive, the teacher is *truly* impressed and, indeed, might learn something new themselves. The only real "superiority" the teachers have is extra knowledge in some interesting or useful discipline. Nothing more. Manifestations of authority and power have no place in the relationship.

And in the end, respect brings respect, resulting in a situation in which students may actually *realize* these high expectations, often in surprising ways. Those few successful teachers know the truth of this. How did they learn it? Perhaps by trial and error? More probably by instinct. I don't know. I wish I knew. But I do know that teachers who combine these three qualities will, in their own small way, move their students closer to one of the ultimate goals of a lifetime: a passion for learning.

/ High-Jumping

Of all the formulations of play, the briefest and the best is to be found in Plato's LAWS. He sees the model of true playfulness in the need of all young creatures, animal and human, to leap. To truly leap you must learn how to use the ground as a springboard, and how to land resiliently and safely. It means to test the leeway allowed by given limits; to outdo and yet not escape gravity.[56]

—Erik Erikson

amily rumor has it that, somewhere, there's a photo of my grandfather (as a young boy), high-jumping in the backyard of his home in Blue Mound, Illinois. Someday, I'd like to see this picture, for it connects him with me. You see, I love to high-jump, too.

In fact, jumping has been a minor passion of mine since grade school. Just about everywhere I have ever lived, I have constructed a set of crude high-jump standards and have somewhere located a suitable crossbar. That's pretty much all one needs, except for a soft place to land.

Before you get the wrong impression, however, I should confess right off that, despite my obsession with this sport,

I'm not a very good jumper. In fact, most highschoolers today, who jump only as high as I do, would probably not make it to the regional track meet. A while back, our nine-year-old son asked me (quite honestly, I'm sure) if I was "approaching the world's record." (He'd like to be proud of his dad, if for no reason than to brag to his friends.) But now he knows the truth, as verified by his own copy of *The Guinness Book of World Records*, that his father jumps more than *three feet* below what the best jumpers can do. Not very impressive. If my memory is correct, I actually jumped slightly higher in the ninth or tenth grade; but, even there, I never made the track and field team.

Enjoyment as Motivation

I'm often haunted by the thought that if I had made the high-school team or been forced to jump in a physical education class, I'd probably now have little, if any, interest in high-jumping. I am intrigued, for example, by George Sheehan's question, "What happened to our play on our way to becoming adults?" and his answer:

> *Downgraded by the intellectuals, dismissed by the economists, put aside by the psychologists, it was left to the teachers to deliver the coup de grace. Physical education was born and turned what was joy into boredom, what was fun into drudgery, what was pleasure into work.*[57]

One might speculate what other amateur enjoyments and later-life pleasures were also ruined by schooling.

Thus, it is not for achievement, honor, or record heights that I jump. I jump simply because I enjoy it. First I enjoy thinking about the jump beforehand, then translating the thought into action—slowly running toward the bar, speeding up on the last step or two—and, in a flash, hurtling myself over.

Sometimes, I experiment with different speeds, different steps, different zones of concentration. Like any other sport, high-jumping can be infinitely complicated or wonderfully simple. The purely analytical side is interesting; but more fun is the sense of abandon, of letting go. Of course, I have yet to feel anything grandiose. For me, there has been no Zen *satori*, no ecstasies to report back. Yet, I can honestly say that, once or twice, I've actually felt like I was—well, *flying* (if only for an instant). It was not unlike that wonderful sensation I once felt, when young, in dreams. I've also been able to jump without thinking of anything in particular—just feeling my feet against dirt, wind and sun on my back, and, at the same time, listening to the intermittent crows, crickets (great jumpers themselves!); and, off in the distance, hearing the call of a mourning dove. All the while loping toward the bar; then the sudden *spring*—converting horizontal momentum into vertical flight.

JUMPING STYLES

To jump any reasonable height takes balance, rhythm, coordination, and good form. My jumping style is the old-fashioned Western Roll first perfected by Stanford jumper, George Horne in 1912. It is a technique that takes more time to learn than the easy "Scissors," or the simple "Straddle" (jumping as if you had tried to leap up onto a horse's back and wound up on the other side!), or even the relatively recent backward leap called the "Fosbury Flop."

In jumping the Western Roll, you take off from your inside foot while kicking your outside foot as hard and as high as you can. As your kicking leg approaches the bar, your body and take-off leg quickly rise to join the upper leg so that everything "rolls" over pretty much at the same time. A photograph taken at the instant of clearance shows the jumper "lying" on his or her side (parallel to the bar) with the kicking leg stretched out and the take-off leg slightly tucked in near the bar. Unlike some of the other styles, such as the Scissors or Straddle, here everything goes over the bar simultaneously, thus enhancing the sensation of "flying."

I was somewhat surprised to learn that no recent athlete has broken the world's high-jump record using this technique. But in 1912, Horne cleared 6 feet, 7 inches (a record for his era); while more recently, Gene Johnson made a little over 7 feet using the Roll. However, today's best jumpers, using the Flop or Straddle, are now jumping eight feet or more!

A GOOD JUMP

Let me repeat once again—I jump because I like to jump. I have jumped in the rain, and I've jumped when there was snow on the ground. Sometimes, I'll jump when I don't feel very well. Often I've discovered that *the way* I jump tells me something about my physical or mental state. I've also discovered that high-jumping can be an interesting exercise in learning to confront fear. Anytime you jump at chest level or above, you're obviously taking some physical risk. There the metal bar sits unwavering, inelastic, and uncompromisingly hard. The bar I currently use is made of an aluminum alloy, triangular in shape, and has sharp edges. If my knee hits it, it can be quite painful. I've also sprained my jumping foot; and it is not unusual for me to hurt my back or wrist.

Also remember that a good jump puts you many feet into the air; and, sooner or later, you must return to the earth. Yet, I've discovered that it's impossible to make a satisfying jump when I have even the slightest air of caution about me. To put it another way, at the moment of take-off, I must give in, or surrender, to an instantaneous intuition. A good jump, in short, involves a kind of faith that everything *will* go perfectly. Yet, as often happens, a speck of fear intrudes at the last moment, forcing me either to abort or make a miserable and often painful jump. (Could this, I wonder, be some kind of metaphor for life?)

So, perhaps, now you understand why I keep jumping. It's somehow wrapped up in power, form, surrender and, sometimes, the feeling of flight. Perhaps, someday, it might even be more than that.

Why couldn't high-jumping (or any other similar sport) evolve into a more perfect state, such as the famous martial arts of Japan? Why couldn't we experience (after sufficient skill development and concentration), something that is equivalent to what archer Eugen Herrigel describes in his book, *Zen In The Art Of Archery*, as a state of

> *serene pulsation...which can be heightened into the feeling, otherwise, experienced only in rare dreams, of extraordinary lightness, and in the rapturous certainty of being able to summon up energies in any direction.*[58]

It's surely something to look forward to. But in the meantime, for me at least, I'll continue my unspectacular leaps. With friendly crickets at hand, thoughts of childhood

or Grandpa Bauer jumping in Blue Mound; with corn
rustling in the garden, spruce nearby, grass bending in the
wind, the sun disappears behind a cloud, and I'm off.

/ Notes

1. Joanna Macy, "Listening to the Beings of the Future," *New Age*, January/February 1991, p. 36.

2. J. Baird Callicot, ed., *Companion to A Sand County Almanac*, (Madison: The University of Wisconsin Press, 1987), p. 286.

3. Aldo Leopold, *A Sand County Almanac*, (London: Oxford University Press) 1949, pp. 201-226.

4. Janet Raloff, "CO_2: How Will We Spell Relief?" *Science News*, December 24 and 31, 1988, p. 133.

5. Quoted from Elizabeth Drew, *Poetry, A Modern Guide to Its Understanding and Enjoyment* (New York: Dell, 1959), pp. 19–20.

6. Robert M. Pirsig, *Zen and the Art of Motorcycle Maintenance* (New York: Bantam, 1974), p. 91.

7. Henry David Thoreau, *Walden* (New York: Bramall House, 1951), p. 348.

8. Norman Ware, *The Industrial Worker 1840-1860* (Gloucester, MA: Peter Smith, 1959), p. viii.

9. Ibid., p. 45.

10. Gerald F. Seib, "Recessions Cause Death Rate to Rise," *The Wall Street Journal,* May 25, 1980, p. 17.

11. Meg Cox, "On Their Own," *The Wall Street Journal,* September 15, 1981, p. 1.

12. Peter Drucker, *Management* (New York: Harper & Row, 1974), p. 261.

13. *Walden,* p. 19.

14. Ibid., p. 19.

15. Henry David Thoreau, *The Journal of Henry David Thoreau,* ed. by R. Torrey, F. Allen (New York: Dover, 1962), Journal entry from July 5th, 1852.

16. *Walden,* p. 67.

17. Ibid., p. 66.

18. Ibid., 68.

19. Ibid., p. 51.

20. *Journal,* May 6th, 1851.

21. *Walden,* p. 148.

22. Ibid., p. 337.

23. Walter Harding, *The Days of Henry David Thoreau* (New York: Dover, 1982), p. 286.

24. *Walden,* p. 106.

25. Ibid., p. 106.

26. Ibid., p. 29.

27. *Journal,* July 19th, 1851.

28. *Walden,* p. 86.

29. Ibid., p. 45.

30. Wade Green and Soma Golden, "Luddites Were Not All Wrong," *New York Times Magazine,* November 26, 1979, p. 24.

31. Adam Smith, *Wealth of Nations,* Vol. 1 (New York: J.M. Dent & Sons, 1910), p. 72.

32. Irving Kristol, "The Worst is Yet to Come," *The Wall Street Journal*, November 26, 1979, p. 24.

33. Mel Ellis, "The Good Earth," *Milwaukee Journal*, March 3, 1974.

34. E.B. White, *The Points of My Compass* (New York: Harper, 1962), p. 67.

35. Henry Caudill, *My Land is Dying* (New York: Dutton, 1971), p. 104.

36. James A. Michener, *The Quality of Life* (New York: Lippincott, 1970), pp. 86-87

37. Christopher Williams, *Craftsman of Necessity* (New York: Vintage, 1974), p. 91.

38. B. Coburn, "Nepali Aama," *The Coevolutionary Quarterly*, Spring 1980, pp. 104-105.

39. Rex Roberts, Your Engineered House (New York: M. Evans and Co., 1964). *See also* Ken Kern, *The Owner Built Home* (New York: Charles Scribner's Sons, 1975).

40. Quoted from: W.C. Ellerbroek, M.D., "Language, Thought, & Disease," *The Coevolutionary Quarterly*, Spring, 1978, p. 31.

41. Lewis Thomas, *The Medusa and the Snail* (New York: Bantam, 1979), p. 39.

42. Milton Friedman (with the assistance of Rose Friedman), *Capitalism and Freedom* (Chicago: University of Chicago Press, 1962).

43. Ivan Illich, *DeSchooling Society* (New York: Harper and Row, 1971), p. 12.

44. *Wealth of Nations*, p. 110.

45. Marcia D. Lowe, *State of the World–1992*, (New York: W.W. Norton, 1992), pp. 126-127. *See also* "Helping Nature Heal," special issue, *The Whole Earth Review*, Spring, 1990; also

see Malcom Margolin's fine book on restoring land entitled *The Earth Manual* (Berkeley: Heyday Books, 1985).

46. Ibid.

47. Lester R. Brown, *State of the World–1992*, (New York: W.W. Norton, 1992), pp. 174-175.

48. Thich Nhat Hanh, *Peace is Every Step* (New York: Bantam, 1991), pp. 95-96; 105-106.

49. Bill McKibben, *The End of Nature* (New York: Random House, 1989), p. 18.

50. Ibid. p. 18.

51. *Economic Report of the President* (1990), p. 221.

52. Peter Raven, "One-Fifth of Earth's Species Face Extinction," *U.S.A. Today*, June 6, 1986, p. 5.

53. James Lovelock, "Only Man's Presence Can Save Nature," *Harpers*, April, 1990, p. 47.

54. Rishworth M. Kiddar, "Let's Not Wait for 'Proof' on Warning of Global Warming," *The Christian Science Monitor*, June 27, 1988. *See also,* Wallace S. Broecker's "Global Warming on Trial," *Natural History*, April, 1992, p. 6.

55. Lao Tzu, *The Way of Life*, Translated by Witter Bynner, (New York: Capricorn Books, 1944), p. 65.

56. Erik H. Erikson, *Toys and Reasons* (New York: Norton, 1977).

57. George A. Sheehan, *Dr. Sheehan on Running* (Mountain View, CA: World Publishers, 1975), p. 190.

58. Eugen Herigel, *Zen in the Art of Archery* (New York: Vintage, 1971), p. 41.

/ ABOUT THE AUTHOR

James Eggert, teacher and writer, has been on the staff of the University of Wisconsin-Stout (Menomonie, WI) since 1968. He also served in the U.S. Peace Corps working with Kenyans on a land-reform program from 1964-66. His current books include *Invitation to Economics, What is Economics?* (Bristlecone/Mayfield), and *Low-Cost Earth Shelters* (Stackpole). *Meadowlark Economics* is a collection from previously published pieces.